TODAY
is the DAY...

TODAY
is the DAY...

... everyday insights for an *extraordinary* life

Christian
LIFE
A STRANG COMPANY

Most CHRISTIAN LIFE products are available at special quantity discounts for bulk purchase for sales promotions, premiums, fund-raising, and educational needs. For details, write Christian Life, 600 Rinehart Road, Lake Mary, Florida 32746, or telephone (407) 333-0600.

TODAY is the DAY
Published by Christian Life
A Strang Company
600 Rinehart Road
Lake Mary, Florida 32746

www.charismahouse.com

Scripture quotations marked GNT are from the Good News Translation, Second Edition. Copyright © 1992 by the American Bible Society. Used by permission.

Scripture quotations marked NAS are taken from the New American Standard Bible, Updated. Copyright © 1960, 1962, 1963, 1968, 1971, 1972, 1973, 1975, 1977, 1995 by the Lockman Foundation. Used by permission. (www.Lockman.org)

Scripture quotations marked NIrV are from the Holy Bible: New International Reader's Version. Copyright © 1995, 1996, 1998 by the International Bible Society. Used by permission.

Scripture quotations marked NIV are from the Holy Bible: New International Version. Copyright © 1973, 1978, 1984, by the International Bible Society. Used by permission.

Scripture quotations marked NKJV are from the New King James Version of the Bible. Copyright © 1979, 1980, 1982 by Thomas Nelson, Inc., publishers. Used by permission.

Scripture quotations marked NRSV are from the New Revised Standard Version of the Bible. Copyright © 1989 by the Division of Christian Education of the National Council of the Churches of Christ in the USA. Used by permission.

Cover design by Whisner Design Group, Tulsa, Oklahoma

ISBN 10:   1-59979-271-0
ISBN 13:   978-1-59979-271-2

BISAC Category: Religion/Christian Life/Inspirational

First Edition
08 09 10 11 12—9 8 7 6 5 4 3 2 1

Printed in the United States of America

All who call on God in true faith,
earnestly from the heart, will
certainly be heard, and will receive
what they have asked and desired.

MARTIN LUTHER

Let us pursue the things which make
for peace and the things by which
one may edify another.

Romans 14:19, NKJV

TODAY *is the* DAY...

Contents

Rekindle Your Resolve

Take Care of Yourself

Give God Control

Live to the Fullest

Love Others

Pursue Your Dreams

TODAY *is the* DAY...

Introduction

Behold, I will do a new thing, now it
shall spring forth; shall you not know it?
I will even make a road in the
wilderness and rivers in the desert.

Isaiah 43:19, NKJV

*G*od is ready to do wonderful things in, for, and through you. And He is ready to do this starting now. *Today is the Day* offers you gentle but powerful thoughts and affirmations for making positive changes in your life. An inspiring quote, a simple affirmation, and a life-changing scripture verse can set the tone of your day. They will help you attune your attitudes and actions to creating a happier, more fulfilling spiritual life starting now.

Today is the Day challenges you to deepen your relationship with God, make a difference in the lives of others, and become the person God meant you to be. Simple actions taken now can change the course of your life. Today is the first day of the rest of your life. How do you want to live it?

Always be in a state of expectancy and see that
you leave room for God to come in as he likes.

OSWALD CHAMBERS

*The faithful person lives
constantly with God.*

SAINT CLEMENT OF ALEXANDRIA

*There is an appointed time for
everything. And there is a time
for every event under heaven.*

Ecclesiastes 3:1, NAS

TODAY
is the DAY...
To Keep Your Good Name

A good name is to be chosen rather than great riches,
loving favor rather than silver and gold.

Proverbs 22:1, NKJV

*T*here is no replacement for a good reputation. Talk and credentials can get a person only so far, and a good reputation cannot be overestimated. If you are eager to move ahead, heed the Bible and make building a strong reputation a priority. Do not bother to try to convince others how good you are—simply prove it by being good. Live every day of your life as if it matters, and take telling—and living—the truth seriously. There is great joy in knowing that you have chosen to live by God's priorities.

A good name is better than fine perfume.

Ecclesiastes 7:1, NIV

Glass, china, and reputation are easily
crack'd and never well mended.

BENJAMIN FRANKLIN

TODAY
is the **DAY**...

To Move Past Your Mistakes

*You will be able to know the will of God—what is
good and is pleasing to him and is perfect.*

Romans 12:2, GNT

It is human to make mistakes. The real problem comes
when you allow those mistakes to take you in the wrong
direction. Once you start down a certain road, it is difficult to admit that you are going the wrong way and then
to turn around. But regardless of how difficult turning
around may be, you will never be sorry when you choose
to correct your mistakes rather than to compound them.
God is always there to give you the courage you need to set
a new path and go on.

*If you listen to advice and are willing to learn,
one day you will be wise.*

Proverbs 19:20, GNT

*The man who makes no mistakes does
not usually make anything.*
WILLIAM CONNOR MAGEE

TODAY
is the **DAY...**

To Plan for Success

Commit to the LORD whatever you do,
and your plans will succeed.

Proverbs 16:3, NIV

*Y*ou can learn about success from books, speakers, and dozens of sources. They can help you with practical plans for succeeding. Learn from them, and commit to making a plan for creating a successful life. But remember that God is the best teacher you will ever have. What matters most is God's formula for success, spelled out in Proverbs 16:3. The formula is this: talk to God, seek His will, ask Him to bless your plans, and then commit them to His care and direction for success in carrying them out.

May he give you the desire of your heart
and make all your plans succeed.

Psalm 20:4, NIV

One of the biggest factors in success is
the courage to undertake something.

JAMES A. WORSHAM

TODAY
is the DAY...

To Be Diligent at Work

The plans of people who work hard succeed.
Proverbs 21:5, NIrV

*A*s the lowly ant demonstrates, life is a roll-up-your-sleeves proposition. God gives you the basic ingredients you need for your daily bread, but He expects you to do the baking. You can have lots of enthusiasm for the final product—a warm, tasty loaf of bread—but unless you are willing to do the work required to produce it, enthusiasm will not get you very far. When it comes to the tasks that lay ahead, roll up your sleeves and get to work. Diligent effort produces the satisfaction of a job well done.

*Hands that work hard will rule. But people who
don't want to work will become slaves.*

Proverbs 12:24, NIrV

---

*For the diligent the week has seven todays;
for the slothful seven tomorrows.*

AUTHOR UNKNOWN

TODAY *is the* DAY...

To Stand Firm

When the storm has swept by, the wicked are gone,
but the righteous stand firm forever.

Proverbs 10:25, NIV

*E*ndurance is simply pushing yourself a little farther than you think you can go and then doing it again. And again. And again. Life offers plenty of opportunities to surrender in the face of difficulty. The key to endurance in the struggle to do the right thing is to lean on God's support in difficult and dangerous times. Trust in this moment, right now. Know that God is with you in each situation, and trust that He will give you the courage and strength to stand firm.

If you endure when you do right and suffer for it,
you have God's approval.

1 Peter 2:20, NRSV

> *To endure is the first thing that a child*
> *ought to learn, and that which he will*
> *have the most need to know.*
>
> JEAN JACQUES ROUSSEAU

TODAY
is the DAY...
To Lead by Example

Take care of a fig tree and you will have figs to eat.
Servants who take care of their master will be honored.

Proverbs 27:18, GNT

*W*hether you are at work or with a group in which you
volunteer, realize that your words and actions have the
potential to impact how people view the total organiza-
tion. In contrast, you can also close communication with
a patron through a thoughtless gesture or careless comment. You cannot overlook your involvement in the success of the group. Realize that you have a greater influence
on others than you know. Choose to make that influence
a positive one. Be willing to lead others by setting an example
of love.

Before destruction one's heart is haughty,
but humility goes before honor.

Proverbs 18:12, NRSV

Next to doing a good job yourself the greatest
joy is in having someone else do a first-class
job under your direction.

WILLIAM FEATHER

TODAY
is the DAY...
To Live with Integrity

Honest weights and scales are the LORD's;
all the weights in the bag are His work.

Proverbs 16:11, NKJV

*P*eople notice when you demonstrate integrity in your choices and actions; you do not have to say a word. The best advertisement any business can receive is word of mouth. Nevertheless, the opposite is also true—one negative experience will be told many times over. God requires man to strive to live by His standards of honest scales and balances. These standards will honor God and demonstrate His love to others. To the best of your ability, honor God by living with integrity and serving the highest good for all concerned.

The integrity of the upright will guide them, but the
crookedness of the treacherous will destroy them.

Proverbs 11:3, NAS

> *To be employed in things connected with virtue*
> *is most agreeable with the character and*
> *inclinations of an honest man.*
>
> JOHN WOOLMAN

TODAY
is the DAY...
To Be a Leader

When the righteous are in authority, the people rejoice.
Proverbs 29:2, NRSV

Whether you are the president of the United States or a supervisor of a couple of employees, God can provide the wisdom and guidance you need to be a successful leader. Being a leader is only partially dependent upon your skills and intelligence. The true character of a leader is demonstrated in his morals, his commitment to truth and fairness, and his ability to communicate direction. Ultimately, the success of a leader rests on a leader's dependence on God and his willingness to yield his decisions to God's leadership.

When the storm is over, sinners are gone.
But those who do right stand firm forever.

Proverbs 10:25, NIrV

If you do not pray, everything can disappoint you by going wrong. If you do pray, everything can still go wrong, but not in a way that will disappoint you.

HUBERT VAN ZELLER

TODAY
is the DAY...
To Be Creative

The heart of the prudent acquires knowledge,
and the ear of the wise seeks knowledge.

Proverbs 18:15, NKJV

*I*nventors seek to change the world in which they live as they endeavor to find new approaches. Invention, however, is not just for mechanical or intellectual geniuses. God wants every person to continue learning—to continue asking questions and dreaming new ideas. Differing viewpoints allow you to acquire insight into problems and to help generate possible solutions. Differing viewpoints allow you to incorporate the ideas of others into your efforts or to let their words spark a fresh concept within you. Cultivate creativity by being open to new ideas.

I applied my heart to what I observed and
learned a lesson from what I saw.

Proverbs 24:32, NIV

Intelligence is not something possessed once for all. It is in constant process....Its retention requires constant alertness in observing consequences, and an open-minded will to learn.

JOHN DEWEY

TODAY
is the **DAY...**

To Reach for Greatness

*Pride goes before destruction,
and a haughty spirit before a fall.*

Proverbs 16:18, NKJV

*Y*ou may become successful in your career and capable of accomplishing great recognition. If arrogance sneaks in, you may become careless or demonstrate poor judgment. The strongest, most accomplished person continues learning throughout his entire lifetime. He often asks questions, acquires new skills, and weighs advice. Be open to new ideas and ask God to help you cultivate personal greatness. Then you can become the person God created you to be. And you will make a positive contribution, bringing the gift of a great heart to everything you do.

*We are His workmanship, created in Christ Jesus
for good works, which God prepared beforehand
that we should walk in them.*

Ephesians 2:10, NKJV

---

*In humility alone lies true greatness, and that
knowledge and wisdom are profitable
only in so far as our lives are governed by them.*

NICHOLAS OF CUSA

TODAY *is the* DAY...

TO

Plan for Success

·

Live with Integrity

·

Reach for Greatness

·

Rise Above the Circumstance

·

Sow Seeds of Success

·

Apply Your Skills

·

Live Like It Matters

·

Move Beyond Life's Disappointments

·

Remain Optimistic

Conscience is the inner voice that warns us
that someone might be looking.

H. L. MENCKEN

*The good person out of the good treasure
of the heart produces good.*

Luke 6:45, NRSV

TODAY
is the DAY...

To Rise Above the Circumstance

*Fools show their anger at once,
but the prudent ignore an insult.*

Proverbs 12:16, NRSV

*W*hen circumstances seem to be against you, do not give in and allow them to defeat you. You are called by God to be better than the circumstances, and He can help you rise above them. Instead of being angry or depressed, take time to pray. Then look for new options, different ideas, and more powerful ways of reacting to what is happening around you. Do what you can to make a bad situation better. With God's help, you can rise above the current circumstance and bring good out of evil.

*Do not fear, for I am with you, do not be afraid, for I am
your God; I will strengthen you, I will help you, I will
uphold you with my victorious right hand.*

Isaiah 41:10, NRSV

> *God, give us grace to accept with serenity the things that cannot be
> changed, courage to change the things which should be changed,
> and the wisdom to distinguish the one from the other.*
>
> REINHOLD NIEBUHR

TODAY
is the DAY...

To Serve with Love

God is able to give you more than you need, so that you
will always have all you need for yourselves and
more than enough for every good cause.

2 Corinthians 9:8, GNT

*T*here are many ways to love and serve God. You can serve
through good works. But all service is not equal. The service that means the most to God is that which is given in
love, freely and generously. Love does not count wrongs,
but looks for what is right. Loving service sees a need and
meets it without fanfare or need for applause. Today is the
day to serve with love, knowing that human beings may
judge by what gets done, but God sees the motivations of
the heart.

If someone says, "I love God," and hates his brother, he is a
liar; for he who does not love his brother whom he has seen,
how can he love God whom he has not seen?

1 John 4:20, NKJV

> *Your neighbor is the man who is next to you at the*
> *moment, the man whom any business has*
> *brought you into contact.*
>
> GEORGE MACDONALD

TODAY
is the DAY...
To Sow Seeds of Success

*A hard-working farmer has plenty to eat, but it is
stupid to waste time on useless projects.*

Proverbs 12:11, GNT

*T*he time and energy it takes to grow a vegetable garden can be compared to the effort it takes to grow your life. Fill your life with healthy, nourishing influences. Be careful of what you read, what you listen to, whom you talk with, where you go, and whom you choose for friends. Sow seeds of success in good work completed, done with a good will and a good attitude. Sow seeds of dreams by paying attention to what you love to do and by nurturing your unique gifts and talents.

*He who gathers in summer is a son who acts wisely, but
he who sleeps in harvest is a son who acts shamefully.*

Proverbs 10:5, NAS

---

*We plough the fields and scatter the good seed on the land,
but it is fed and watered by God's Almighty hand.*

JANE MONTGOMERY CAMPBELL

TODAY
is the DAY...

To Refocus Your Mind

*Those who live as their human nature tells them to, have
their minds controlled by what human nature wants.
Those who live as the Spirit tells them to, have their
minds controlled by what the Spirit wants.*

Romans 8:5, GNT

Philippians 4:8 urges you to focus your thoughts on things
that are true, noble, right, pure, lovely, admirable, excellent, and praiseworthy. What you think about is what you
become. You can choose what to focus on. You can focus
on negativity, or you can focus on what is good and right
and perfect. If you are struggling with unproductive,
destructive thoughts, ask God to help you practice the
pattern for good thinking outlined in Philippians. With
God's help you can renew and transform your mind, one
thought at a time.

The thoughts of the righteous are right.

Proverbs 12:5, NKJV

---

*Occupy your minds with good thoughts,
or the enemy will fill them with bad ones.*

SIR THOMAS MORE

TODAY
is the DAY...
To Take the Lead

Those who lead others to do what is right are wise.
Proverbs 11:30, NIrV

*E*ven if you consider yourself a follower rather than a leader, there are times when you have to take the lead. If you have the courage and faith to try, that is all God asks. Do not be afraid to take that first step of faith and lead the way. Although it is true that God bestows certain people with extraordinary leadership gifts, you, too, can serve as a leader when God sets a challenge before you. Trust Him to guide you, and freely accept the responsibility when it comes your way.

Remember those who led you, who spoke the word of God to you; and considering the result of their conduct, imitate their faith.

Hebrews 13:7, NAS

Christian leadership . . . appears to break down into five main ingredients—clear vision, hard work, dogged perseverance, humble service and iron discipline.
JOHN R. W. STOTT

TODAY
is the DAY...

To Apply Your Skills

Do you see those who are skillful in their work?
They will serve kings.

Proverbs 22:29, NRSV

You have certain gifts, talents, and skills. Some you have developed, some you have neglected, and some you have yet to develop. Your skills and talents are needed. Today is a good day to take an inventory of your skills. What gifts can you give today to help others and to improve their lives? What skills can you hone to reach your fullest potential? What talents are lying dormant that need to be revived? Ask God how you can apply your skills and use them for the highest good of all.

Whatever you do, do your work heartily,
as for the Lord rather than for men.

Colossians 3:23, NAS

Every job is a self-portrait of the person who did it.
Autograph your work with excellence.

AUTHOR UNKNOWN

TODAY
is the **DAY...**

To Live Like It Matters

The fruit that godly people bear is like a tree of life.
Proverbs 11:30, NIrV

*T*he world will tell you that what you do is not important. But who you are, what you do, and how you live your life is important to God. You may never know how something you do in a moment will affect someone for a lifetime, so be sure that you make your moments count. Live your life as if it matters, knowing that with God's help, you can make a positive difference in the world today. Above all, make sure that the seeds you plant bear something beautiful and good.

We pray . . . that you may live a life worthy of the Lord and may please him in every way: bearing fruit in every good work, growing in the knowledge of God.

Colossians 1:10, NIV

You have to sow before you can reap.
You have to give before you can get.
ROBERT COLLIER

TODAY
is the DAY...

To Know What Counts

Some people pretend to be rich but have nothing.
Others pretend to be poor but have great wealth.

Proverbs 13:7, NIrV

*N*ot everything that counts can be counted. There is no intrinsic virtue to being poor and struggling; on the other hand, neither is being wealthy a sure sign of God's blessing. God's concern is your heart; He is more interested in developing character in your life than in enlarging your bank account. The most important thing, now and always, is to love God with all your heart and to pass those values on to those you influence. Having money is not the issue. Loving God is.

Command people who are rich in this world not to be proud.
Tell them not to put their hope in riches. Wealth is so
uncertain. Command those who are rich to put their hope
in God. He richly provides us with everything to enjoy.

1 Timothy 6:17, NIrV

Money was made not to command our will,
but all our lawful pleasures to fulfill.
ABRAHAM COWLEY

TODAY
is the **DAY...**

To Do the Right Thing

*All Scripture is inspired by God and is useful for teaching
the truth, rebuking error, correcting faults,
and giving instruction for right living.*

2 Timothy 3:16 GNT

*P*eace of mind and a clear conscience are precious commodities, and they cannot be bought at any price. They are yours only when you determine day-by-day, hour-by-hour, minute-by-minute to do the right thing no matter what. God honors the person who is willing to do the right thing with integrity and a willing heart. Even when you fall short—as everyone does—God is quick to forgive. Be strong and faithful. He is always there to help you do the right thing.

*Do what is right and fair. The LORD accepts
that more than sacrifices.*

Proverbs 21:3, NIrV

> *A man's first care should be to avoid
> the reproaches of his own heart.*
>
> JOSEPH ADDISON

TODAY
is the **DAY...**

To Go Past Disappointments

A longing fulfilled is a tree of life.
Proverbs 13:12, NIV

*W*hen disappointments come, do not let resentment make you miserable and sour your attitude about life. That is a sure recipe for making a bad situation worse. But there is a better way. You can choose to release your disappointment and move on. Sometimes a disappointment turns out to be a blessing in disguise. A door closes, and another door opens. A lesson is learned that provides the impetus for new growth and understanding. When you suffer a disappointment, give it to God and trust Him to help you grow from your experience.

The path of life leads upward for the wise.
Proverbs 15:24, NAS

> *Faith is often strengthened right at
> the place of disappointment.*
> RODNEY MCBRIDE

TODAY *is the* **DAY...**

To Put Fear Behind You

The LORD will be your confidence.
Proverbs 3:26, NAS

*F*ear can be faced and left behind. It is your misunderstanding of fear's purpose and lack of faith to deal with it that can get you into trouble. Simply put, fear's function is to warn you of danger, not make you afraid to face it. When fear haunts you, recognize the danger that it represents, and then put your faith into full gear to face it. It takes practice, but as your faith glows brighter, you will find yourself being empowered to deal with it. That is God's promise.

Whoever listens to [wisdom] will live in safety
and be at ease, without fear of harm.

Proverbs 1:33, NIV

> *Many of our fears are tissue paper thin, and a*
> *single courageous step would carry us through them.*
> BRENDAN FRANCIS

TODAY
is the DAY...

To Have Faith

*Your hand will lead me, and Your
right hand will lay hold of me.*

Psalm 139:10, NAS

*S*ometimes walking with God means holding His hand in the dark. You may not see very far ahead, but there is wisdom and guidance in walking trustfully, step-by-step. Each small step of faith is a giant leap of the spirit, responding to the light you already have, discovering that the next step of faith is given at the right and perfect time. You are not alone in those dark times when you are wondering which way to go. God walks beside you, and He knows the path ahead.

*Your faith, then, does not rest on human
wisdom but on God's power.*

1 Corinthians 2:5, GNT

*Faith is not without worry or care,
but faith is fear that has said a prayer.*

AUTHOR UNKNOWN

TODAY
is the **DAY...**

To Remain Optimistic

Be strong and let your heart take courage,
all you who hope in the LORD.

Psalm 31:24, NAS

*M*edical studies consistently find that people who are hopeful are at less risk for disease—and heal more quickly—than those who are not. In these unsettling days, there are many things in the world that can chip away at your hope. But rejoice, God has provided a solid basis for being optimistic about your future. Joy, peace, and love are in His plans for you. He has your good in mind. God invites you daily to claim that hope. The bonus is that hope is also good for your health.

The LORD takes pleasure in those who fear Him,
in those who hope in His mercy.

Psalm 147:11, NKJV

In hope we count on the possibilities of the future and we
do not remain imprisoned in the institutions of the past.

JÜRGEN MOLTMANN

TODAY
is the DAY...
To Choose Your Thoughts

The thoughts of the righteous are just.
Proverbs 12:5, NRSV

Your thoughts are powerful. In truth, every one of your actions starts with a thought. That is why it is important to make your thoughts work for you rather than against you. With God's help, you can choose the thoughts that focus on possibilities, not problems. You will discover that positive thinking can create a positive attitude. You can allow your thoughts to build you up or tear you down. Commit your thoughts to God and choose to think great and hopeful thoughts that can change your world for the better.

A tranquil mind gives life to the flesh.
Proverbs 14:30, NRSV

Change your thoughts and you change your world.
NORMAN VINCENT PEALE

TODAY
is the **DAY...**

To Commit Yourself to Grow

*Give me wisdom and knowledge,
because I trust in your commands.*

Psalm 119:66, GNT

O rville and Wilbur Wright dreamed of flying even as young boys. They studied and experimented and learned everything they could about flying. Today you can fly anywhere because two brothers were dedicated to the task they had resolved to accomplish. They were open to learn and willing to grow in their understanding. Anything worthwhile requires learning, practice, and being on the growing edge before proficiency comes. Commit yourself to personal growth as you seek to reach your goals. God will be there to guide you to triumph.

*I applied my heart to know, to search and seek
out wisdom and the reason of things.*

Ecclesiastes 7:25, NKJV

---

*Every worthwhile accomplishment, big or little, has its stages of
drudgery and triumph; a beginning, a struggle, and a victory.*

AUTHOR UNKNOWN

TODAY
is the DAY...

To Overcome Worry

Worry can rob you of happiness,
but kind words will cheer you up.

Proverbs 12:25, GNT

*W*orry is negative faith. When you worry and imagine worst-case scenarios, you help create the very thing you worry about. Instead of giving your energies to worry, focus on the good already in your life and think about positive possibilities. Remember that God is your source, so anything is possible. You may think you see all the possibilities and probabilities for how a situation can turn out. But God sees the bigger picture and knows how to bring unexpected blessings to you in unexpected ways.

Don't worry about anything. Instead, tell God about
everything. Ask and pray. Give thanks to him.

Philippians 4:6, NIrV

If you love God, you never have to worry again.
PHILLIP DANIEL WATKINS (AGE 7)

TODAY *is the* DAY...

To Remain Constant

Be doers of the word, and not hearers only, deceiving yourselves.
James 1:22, NKJV

*C*onstancy is one vital characteristic that makes God's love trustworthy. God's love for you does not change according to whim or circumstance. His promises and compassion remain steadfast today, tomorrow, and until the end of time. Today you can choose to reflect the character of God by maintaining a constancy of purpose, and remaining faithful to the promises you have made to yourself, to others, and to God. When you are tempted to quit or compromise, remember that God will give you strength to be true to what you believe.

He who is faithful in what is least is faithful also in much.
Luke 16:10, NKJV

Constancy is the foundation of virtue.
FRANCIS BACON

TODAY
is the DAY...

To Be Courageous

Be strong and of good courage, do not fear nor be afraid . . .
for the LORD your God, He is the One who goes with you.
He will not leave you nor forsake you.

Deuteronomy 31:6, NKJV

*I*f you want to accomplish a goal and stay true to your convictions, it is going to take a courageous heart to see it through. You may face opposition, but it does not have to stop you. It takes courage to risk failure, try something new, and persevere in hard times. Almost anything that is worthwhile in life will demand a measure of courage. Remember that God is always with you in these times when your courage is tested. He has helped others, and He will do the same for you.

Let us hold fast the confession of our hope without
wavering, for He who promised is faithful.

Hebrews 10:23, NKJV

Courage is not the absence of fear, but the mastery of fear.
AUTHOR UNKNOWN

TODAY *is the* DAY...

TO

Be Courageous

•

Build a Solid Foundation

•

Consider Your Steps

•

Expand Your Horizons

•

Stop Speaking Negatively

•

Live with Purpose

•

Be a Peacemaker

•

Think Before You Act

•

Choose Words Wisely

A relationship is a living thing.
It needs and benefits from the
same attention to detail that
an artist lavishes on his art.

DAVID VISCOTT

Let us be bold, then, and say, "The Lord is
my helper, I will not be afraid."

Hebrews 13:6, GNT

TODAY
is the DAY...
To Be Confident

Anyone who shows respect for the LORD has a strong tower.
Proverbs 14:26, NIrV

Knowing that God is with you can give you the courage to step out and be who you were created to be. It can give you the courage to fail, then to get up and try again. When fear tries to talk you out of doing something, do not listen. Instead, remind yourself of what God has to say about you—you are more than a conqueror through God who loves you (Romans 8:37). Develop confidence by stepping out in trust, knowing that your confidence is grounded in your faith in God.

The LORD will be your confidence.
Proverbs 3:26, NKJV

Confidence in the natural world is self-reliance,
in the spiritual world it is God-reliance.
OSWALD CHAMBERS

TODAY
is the DAY...

To Put Your Best Foot Forward

Do you see a man skilled in his work? He will stand before kings; he will not stand before obscure men.

Proverbs 22:29, NAS

*G*ive your best effort in everything you do. The way you approach a task shows who you truly are on the inside. It takes character to tackle a job with enthusiasm and stick to it till the work is done. Half-done work makes for a half-lived life. Do your best, and then trust God with the rest. Put your best foot forward, and be generous with your time and energy. You will reap a reward of a job well done and the satisfaction of knowing you did your best.

Your reward depends on what you say and what you do; you will get what you deserve.

Proverbs 12:14, GNT

Your success depends mainly upon what you think of yourself and whether you believe in yourself.

WILLIAM J. H. BOETCKER

TODAY
is the **DAY...**

To Build a Solid Foundation

The fear of the LORD is a fountain of life,
that one may avoid the snares of death.

Proverbs 14:27, NAS

*E*ach day, your life should be built on a solid foundation. Foundation is found in the character of God, and is mirrored to others in your character. The people around you notice how you act and react in various situations. People you do not even know form impressions of your character and integrity just through observation. When you allow God to have control of your life, your attitude and disposition will be different. The challenges of the day will not be able to knock you off your firm footing.

Everyone who comes to Me and hears My words and acts on them, I will show you whom he is like: he is like a man building a house, who dug deep and laid a foundation on the rock; and when a flood occurred, the torrent burst against that house and could not shake it, because it had been well built.

Luke 6:47–48, NAS

The greatest happiness of the greatest number is the foundation of morals and legislation.

JEREMY BENTHAM

TODAY
is the DAY...
To Consider Your Steps

The naive believes everything, but the
sensible man considers his steps.

Proverbs 14:15, NAS

$\mathcal{G}$od has given you the freedom to make your own decisions each day. Sometimes you have a clear blueprint and
know exactly what step is next in the process of creating
your dream. Other times it is not so clear. When you are
not sure of the next step, take time to consider where you
have been and pray about where you want to go. When
you carefully consider your steps, God is able to work in
your life and accomplish His plans and purposes in you.

The steps of a man are established by the LORD,
and He delights in his way. When he falls,
he will not be hurled headlong,
because the LORD is the One
who holds his hand.

Psalm 37:23–24, NAS

No one who accomplished things could expect to avoid mistakes.
Only those who did nothing made no mistakes.

HARRY S. TRUMAN

TODAY
is the **DAY...**

To Expand Your Horizons

*Oh, the depth of the riches both of the wisdom and
knowledge of God! How unsearchable are His
judgments and His ways past finding out!*

Romans 11:33, NKJV

*I*s staying in your personal comfort zone keeping you from branching out and learning something new? If so, you are doing yourself a disservice. Make it a point to find and take advantage of opportunities to learn. God will reward your efforts. Take a class, read a good book, buy a ticket to a show or a lecture, sign up for a workshop, or go to an event like a crafts fair where you can see and learn something new. Expand your horizons with new ideas and experiences. Seek the up-till-now unfamiliar and enjoy the thrill of discovery.

Intelligent people want to learn.

Proverbs 15:14, GNT

---

*Learning is not attained by chance.
It must be sought for with ardor
and attended to with diligence.*

ABIGAIL ADAMS

TODAY
is the DAY...
To Renew Your Vision

Listen, my child, be wise and give
serious thought to the way you live.

Proverbs 23:19, GNT

*T*he path you travel is your choice. If ever in doubt as to
where you should go or what you should do, ask God to
direct you. Open your mind to God, and receive insight
and assurance. Get quiet before Him and leave an open,
quiet space for new thoughts and different ideas to enter.
As you rid yourself of the mental chatter and prejudices,
you can hear the still, small voice of God. It takes courage
to make changes, but a renewed vision helps you live your
life with renewed energy.

The way of the lazy is overgrown with thorns,
but the path of the upright is a level highway.

Proverbs 15:19, NRSV

Lift up thine eyes, and seek
His Face. . . . Christ is the path,
and Christ the prize.

JOHN SAMUEL BEWLEY MONSELL

TODAY
is the DAY...
To Speak Boldly

The righteous are as bold as a lion.
Proverbs 28:1, NIV

*D*o not hesitate to be bold in your convictions, especially when it comes to your faith. The only way some people will ever know the truth is to hear it from you. Trust God for the courage to speak boldly. Ask Him for the right words and the ability to speak them kindly and effectively. Whether you are sharing an experience of faith, or a conviction about what you believe is a right action to take, it is time for you to bravely meet the challenge. Speak the truth with gentle words, sincere concern, and loving compassion.

*My inmost being will rejoice when
your lips speak what is right.*

Proverbs 23:16, NIV

> *Even a mouse can squeak with
> boldness when he stands on the
> shoulders of an elephant.*
>
> DUDLEY ADAMS

TODAY
is the DAY...

To Stop Speaking Negatively

Do everything without complaining or arguing,
so that you may become blameless and pure.

Philippians 2:14–15, NIV

*I*t often feels good, even justified, to gripe and complain, but the most successful people have learned to keep their wits about them. Nothing good ever comes from speaking negatively. It drains your energy. It is better to offer positive, encouraging words or to keep your opinions to yourself until you are in an appropriate environment for addressing certain issues. By finding the best in every situation, however small, you can minimize your frustrations and guarantee that your words will never be the cause of confusion and strife.

There is one who speaks rashly like the thrusts of a sword,
but the tongue of the wise brings healing.

Proverbs 12:18, NAS

> *Wisdom is knowing when to*
> *speak your mind and when*
> *to mind your speech.*
> AUTHOR UNKNOWN

TODAY
is the DAY...
To Live with Purpose

Let reverence for the LORD be the concern of your life.
If it is, you have a bright future.

Proverbs 23:17–18, GNT

Y ou are just you, exactly the way God intended. God knits every individual together in the womb with specific physical characteristics, strengths, weaknesses, talents, and tendencies. Then He gives each person one more thing— purpose. The desire to find your place in the world is a God-given drive that helps you make the most of your own unique role in life. Though some roles receive more public accolades than others, all of God's children have starring roles. You are here at this time and place to fulfill a unique purpose.

[The apostle Paul said,] "I press on toward the goal for the
prize of the heavenly call of God in Christ Jesus."

Philippians 3:14, NRSV

Purpose is what gives life meaning.
A drifting boat always drifts downstream.
CHARLES PARKHURST

TODAY
is the DAY…

To Forgive Those Who Hurt You

Be merciful just as your Father is merciful. . . .
Forgive others, and God will forgive you.

Luke 6:36–37, GNT

*I*magine a perfect world without the pain of betrayal and where no one ever says hurtful things to you or fails you in any way. You cannot make the world perfect, but your choice to forgive the people who hurt you can restore this imperfect world. Forgiveness comes as the touch of human kindness, reaching out with love. Forgiveness keeps love's flame burning and restores hope in any situation. Instead of nursing your wounds or holding others' failings and shortcomings against them, allow love and forgiveness to be your motivation.

Love does not keep a record of wrongs.

1 Corinthians 13:5, GNT

Every person should have a special cemetery lot in which
to bury the faults of friends and loved ones.

AUTHOR UNKNOWN

TODAY
is the DAY...
To Be a Peacemaker

Counselors of peace have joy.
Proverbs 12:20, NAS

*A*t times, it can seem like *peace* is a concept found only in the dictionary. Read the headlines, and you see a world overrun with conflict. Neighborhoods, cities, states, and countries desperately need peace, and yet it will come only with the changed hearts of individuals. Peace is the soft answer that turns away wrath. Peace is the kind act you perform. Peace is forgiving the neighbor who wronged you. Peace is allowing God's peace to reign in your heart. You can be an ambassador of peace to the world—starting now.

God is not a God of disorder but of peace.
1 Corinthians 14:33, NIV

> *Peace is such a precious jewel that I would give anything for it but truth.*
> MATTHEW HENRY

TODAY
is the DAY...

To Show Kindness to Strangers

A woman who has a kind heart gains respect.
Proverbs 11:16, NIrV

*W*hat does it mean to be kind? It means more than just doing kind things. True kindness is a living expression of God's love. And how does God love? Unconditionally. True kindness is seeing a need and meeting it—and not judging the person who is in need. Kindness then becomes a practical way to express your love for God by loving other human beings unconditionally. Kindness sees others as God sees them, and then acts lovingly to live out the priorities of the kingdom of God on earth through simple kind actions.

Be kind and honest and you will live a long life.
Proverbs 21:21, GNT

Be the living expression of God's kindness: kindness in your face, kindness in your eyes, kindness in your smile, kindness in your warm greeting.
MOTHER TERESA

TODAY
is the DAY...
To Think Before You Act

Sensible people always think before they act.
Proverbs 13:16, GNT

*C*ommon sense has been defined as wisdom dressed in
work clothes. God is the source of all wisdom, and He says
in the Bible that He will give wisdom to anyone who asks
for it. By cultivating a regular relationship with God, you
will find that His wisdom helps you see beyond surface
appearances, giving you wisdom to handle every circumstance. If you have found yourself longing for the kind of
common sense that can help you find solutions in life, just
ask God for it.

If any of you lack wisdom, you should pray to God,
who will give it to you; because God gives
generously and graciously to all.

James 1:5, GNT

Fine sense and exalted sense are not
half so useful as common sense.
ALEXANDER POPE

TODAY
is the DAY...

To Weigh Your Motives Carefully

Every man's way is right in his own eyes,
but the LORD weighs the hearts.

Proverbs 21:2, NAS

*W*hy—really—do you do the things you do for others? If you are hoping to look good to someone else, receive some type of reward, acquire control over others, or alleviate guilt, it could be that you need to step back and ask God to help you purify your motives. By moving beyond pleasing others to pleasing God, you will be doing things for the right reasons. When the motives behind your actions are pleasing to God, your efforts will produce good things—eternal things—in your life and the lives of others.

Everything a man does might seem right to him.
But the LORD knows what that man is thinking.

Proverbs 16:2, NIrV

One of the most excellent intentions that we can possibly have in all our actions is to do them because our Lord did them.

SAINT FRANCIS DE SALES

TODAY *is the* DAY...

To Step Back from Anger

Whoever is slow to anger has great understanding.
Proverbs 14:29, NRSV

*A*nger is a powerful emotion that can cloud your judgment. Feeling frustration over others' behaviors can overwhelm you, leading to angry confrontations and words better left unsaid. The next time someone gives you reason to lose your temper or blow a fuse, impose a cooling-off period on yourself. Step back from the situation and give yourself time to regain perspective. God has promised to show you how to respond in ways that will foster long-lasting results. First, though, you must wait for Him to calm your stormy emotions.

He who is slow to anger is better than the mighty,
and he who rules his spirit than he who takes a city.

Proverbs 16:32, NKJV

The two best times to keep your mouth shut are
when you're swimming and when you're angry.

AUTHOR UNKNOWN

TODAY
is the DAY...
To Love Your Enemies

Love your enemies and do good to them;
lend and expect nothing back. . . .
Be merciful just as your Father is merciful.

Luke 6:35–36, GNT

*W*hen people in your life are less than kind, it is human to want to return evil for evil. God offers a radically different approach. The Bible says to pray for your enemies, and it goes even farther—it says to love them. What does loving your enemy mean? It is more than mere tolerance, better than forgiveness. Loving your enemy means being able to understand him as a fellow human being who struggles, and having compassion for his struggle. You can learn from Christ's example the fine art of compassion and forgiveness.

Don't be happy when your enemy falls.
When he trips, don't let your heart be glad.

Proverbs 24:17, NIrV

If we could read the secret history of our enemies, we should find in each life sorrow and suffering enough to disarm all hostilities.
HENRY WADSWORTH LONGFELLOW

TODAY
is the DAY...
To Choose Words Wisely

If you want to stay out of trouble, be careful what you say.
Proverbs 21:23, GNT

*O*nce something is spoken it can never be revised or erased. That is why it is important to take the time to think before you speak. At times, choosing the right words may actually mean choosing to say nothing at all. This can be difficult in the midst of anger or frustration. Ask God to help you make each word a gift to the person who hears it. Ask yourself if what you are going to say is kind, true, or helpful. Remember that words are powerful, so use them wisely. The words you use today impact you and your listeners for all the tomorrows yet to come.

Avoid worldly and empty chatter,
for it will lead to further ungodliness.

2 Timothy 2:16, NAS

> *Words which do not give the light of*
> *Christ increase the darkness.*
> MOTHER TERESA

TODAY
is the DAY...
To Speak the Truth

*Righteous lips are the delight of kings,
and he who speaks right is loved.*

Proverbs 16:13, NAS

*D*id you say anything yesterday in which you may have been less than completely truthful? Sometimes speaking the truth may be difficult. However, when you maintain your integrity and speak truth with kindness and gentleness, you will stand above the crowd. Honesty should never be used as an excuse to belittle or tear down a friend or colleague. Speak the truth in love, but also speak it with sensitivity and kindness. When people know you are truthful, they will trust you. And you will be able to trust yourself.

*The hearts of wise people guide their mouths.
Their words make people want to learn more.*

Proverbs 16:23, NIrV

*Man passes away; generations are but shadows;
there is nothing stable but truth.*
JOSIAH QUINCY

TODAY
is the DAY...

TO

Turn the Other Cheek

•

Understand the Power of Words

•

Transform Your Heart

•

Take the High Road

•

Speak from the Heart

•

Cultivate Humility

•

Be an Encourager

•

Be Honest in Everything

•

Learn from Mistakes

Right wrongs no man.
THEODORE ROOSEVELT

*To do righteousness and justice is more
acceptable to the LORD than sacrifice.*

Proverbs 21:3, NKJV

TODAY
is the DAY...
To Accept Criticism As Advice

Poverty and disgrace are for the one who ignores instruction,
but one who heeds reproof is honored.

Proverbs 13:18, NRSV

*T*hroughout life, a number of people will offer healthy doses of criticism. Some mean to be helpful, yet others only want to belittle you to make themselves feel better. Filter out the barbs and jabs that can serve only to injure your spirit. Then accept and implement what advice is given as constructive criticism. Realize that an impartial friend often has the advantage of seeing the situation from a different perspective. Maturity and success come when you can discern their intention and learn from the perspective and advice of others.

If you pay attention when you are corrected,
you are wise. If you refuse to learn, you are hurting
yourself. If you accept correction, you will become wiser.

Proverbs 15:31–32, GNT

Half an hour's listening is essential except when you
are very busy. Then a full hour is needed.
SAINT FRANCIS DE SALES

TODAY
is the DAY...

To Maintain Composure

He who restrains his words has knowledge, and he who has a cool spirit is a man of understanding.

Proverbs 17:27, NAS

*C*onflicts arise between neighbors, work associates, friends. How you handle these crises is important. Your tendency could be to blow up immediately and to scream and yell. Rarely will this do anything to solve the problem; in fact, it may drive the wedge deeper and encourage retaliation. Learn to treat others the way you would want to be treated—with respect. Listen before you speak. Keep your cool. When both parties keep a calm, even-tempered attitude, you are able to resolve differences and come up with an equitable solution.

Hot tempers cause arguments, but patience brings peace.

Proverbs 15:18, GNT

> *A tart temper never mellows with age, and a sharp tongue is the only edged tool that grows keener with constant use.*
>
> WASHINGTON IRVING

TODAY
is the **DAY...**

To Control Your Temper

Stupid people express their anger openly,
but sensible people are patient and hold it back.

Proverbs 29:11, GNT

*L*osing your temper and blowing up is counterproductive
and unhealthy. Ask God to help you control your temper
when irritations come your way. Staying calm in the midst
of crisis is a mark of maturity, fostering an ability to
observe intuitively, evaluate quickly, and react appropriately.
The next time you start feeling angry, stop talking and
answer these questions: Is my example one I can be proud
of? Is losing my temper really an effective way to achieve
my goals? God can help you cool a hot temper.

If you are patient, you can win an official over to your side.
And gentle words can break a bone.

Proverbs 25:15, NIrV

Nobody will know what you mean by saying
that "God is love" unless you act it as well.

LAWRENCE PEARSALL JACKS

TODAY
is the **DAY…**

To Speak Gentle Words

A gentle answer turns away wrath,
but a harsh word stirs up anger.

Proverbs 15:1, NAS

*P*eople have differing opinions and ideas of how things should be done. Sometimes the conversation can become heated, and you need to respond wisely. When someone is upset or unwilling to hear another viewpoint, do not waste your time trying to convince him of the wisdom of your viewpoint. The best way to respond is with simple, peaceful words. Speaking gentle words defuses anger. If gentle kindness is ineffective, be willing to walk away and give everyone time to cool off. Ask God for wisdom, and know you did your best.

The mind of the righteous ponders how to answer,
but the mouth of the wicked pours out evil.

Proverbs 15:28, NRSV

> *Peace . . . involves mutual respect and confidence between peoples and nations. Like a cathedral, peace must be constructed patiently and with unshakable faith.*
>
> JOHN PAUL II

TODAY
is the DAY...

To Turn the Other Cheek

*Do not seek revenge or bear a grudge against one of
your people, but love your neighbor as yourself.*

Leviticus 19:18, NIV

*R*evenge is a lose-lose proposition. That is why God says
not to engage in it no matter how severe the offense might
be. There are no exceptions, making it clear that a wrong
never justifies another wrong. It cannot and will not
change the circumstances. What it will do is drag you
down to the level—morally, spiritually, and emotionally—
of the offender. When you have been wronged, leave your
hurt and anger in the hands of God. Healing, justice, and
reconciliation come from Him. Trust Him to work it all
together for good.

*Love your enemies and pray for those who persecute you,
that you may be sons of your Father in heaven.*

Matthew 5:44–45, NIV

---

*Never does the human soul appear so strong and noble as
when it forgoes revenge and dares to forgive an injury.*

EDWIN H. CHAPIN

TODAY
is the DAY...

To Make Your Words Count

Those who guard their mouths preserve their lives.
Proverbs 13:3, NRSV

*T*he words you speak have the power to hurt and to heal, to tear down and to build up. What an incredible responsibility God has given you to use your words wisely and effectively. Take the time and effort necessary to ensure that your words are truthful and encouraging. Lace them with hope for the sake of those who feel hopeless. Sprinkle them with wisdom for those who need guidance. Energize them with love for those who have not known love. Speak the truth in love—from your heart.

Set a guard over my mouth, O LORD;
keep watch over the door of my lips.

Psalm 141:3, NIV

Speak clearly, if you speak at all;
carve every word before you let it fall.
OLIVER WENDELL HOLMES

TODAY
is the DAY...
To Know the Power of Words

The tongue of the righteous is choice silver.
Proverbs 10:20, NRSV

*W*ords are powerful. The old children's saying "Sticks and stones may break my bones, but words will never hurt me" is not true. When God created, He spoke the word, and the world was made manifest. When you speak a word of doubt or fear, you feed the doubts and fears you want to avoid. But words of faith have an even greater effect, overcoming all the negative words spoken in the past. Today, use the power of words to create good in your life by affirming a positive faith.

The tongue has the power of life and death,
and those who love it will eat its fruit.
Proverbs 18:21, NIV

If men would only think through what they said, and the effect it would have on those they're speaking to, many problems would be solved before they started.

KENNETH P. WALTERS

TODAY
is the DAY...

To Transform Your Heart

Above all else, guard your heart,
for it is the wellspring of life.

Proverbs 4:23, NIV

*I*t is the heart that knows God most intimately. It is the heart that is the wellspring of life. Allow God to soften and transform your heart with His love. Take time in prayer to examine your heart. It is possible to do the right things for the wrong motives and the wrong things for the right motives. That is why it is important to examine your motives honestly and often to be sure you are pursuing goals that are in line with God's priorities. Open your heart to God's love.

The LORD searches every heart and understands
every motive behind the thoughts.

1 Chronicles 28:9, NIV

In all our actions, God considers the
intention: whether we act for Him or
for some other motive.

SAINT MAXIMUS THE CONFESSOR

TODAY
is the DAY...
To Take the High Road

*Small is the gate and narrow the road that
leads to life, and only a few find it.*

Matthew 7:14, NIV

*S*ometimes life offers you a set of choices. One seems to be the easy way, a superhighway of society's approval that the crowds flock to. Another leads to a higher way, a straight and narrow path that leads away from the crowds. The high road seems more difficult at first. It means practicing forgiveness, making choices that may not be popular, and following your conscience instead of the crowd. But there are rewards in the heights that people below cannot imagine, including inner peace and an intimate relationship with God.

*One who walks in integrity will be safe, but whoever
follows crooked ways will fall into the Pit.*

Proverbs 28:18, NRSV

> *Only he who keeps his eye fixed on the
> far horizon will find his right road.*
> DAG HAMMARSKJÖLD

TODAY
is the DAY...

To Speak from the Heart

*A word aptly spoken is like apples
of gold in settings of silver.*

Proverbs 25:11, NIV

When Jesus shared a complicated spiritual concept, He simplified it by wrapping it in a story. Jesus' stories were about everyday situations His listeners could relate to—wedding banquets, wayward children, vineyards. His stories were simple and clear, and the lessons behind them unforgettable. By tapping into your common experience as a human being, you can communicate from the heart. Then your speaking will be seasoned with a down-to-earth blessing of love. Your words will have more meaning because everyone who listens will know they come from the heart.

The tongues of wise people use knowledge well.

Proverbs 15:2, NIrV

---

*Be humble and gentle in your conversation; and of few words,
I charge you; but always pertinent when you speak.*

WILLIAM PENN

TODAY
is the DAY...
To Cultivate Humility

Humility comes before honor.
Proverbs 18:12, NIV

*I*f you think you know it all, you do not know much. False pride can trip you up, so watch your step. It is wonderful to be proud of what you accomplish, or of the people you love. But to assume you have all the answers—or better answers than anyone else—can be a dangerous trap. The Bible talks about pride going before a fall, so listen, look, and pray for wisdom. God gives the humble-hearted wisdom and guidance. If you cultivate humility and compassionate kindness, you will find grace wherever you go.

God resists the proud, but gives grace to the humble.
James 4:6, NKJV

If you harden your heart with pride,
you soften your brain with it too.
ANCIENT PROVERB

TODAY
is the DAY...
To Stand for Justice

Speak up for people who cannot speak for themselves.
Protect the rights of all who are helpless.

Proverbs 31:8, GNT

$\int$peaking out for justice is not easy to do. It often means going against the majority opinion and enduring the disapproval of others. But the priorities of God's kingdom demand that you have the courage to speak the truth as you see it, and to help those who are oppressed by injustice. Be willing to do what you can to challenge injustice. The life of Jesus Christ has inspired many to stand for justice. He has promised to give you the strength and courage to do the same.

It is not good to show partiality to the wicked,
or to overthrow the righteous in judgment.

Proverbs 18:5, NKJV

True peace is not merely the absence
of tension; it is the presence of justice.

MARTIN LUTHER KING JR.

TODAY
is the DAY...
To Set a New Standard

Don't say, "I'll get even with you for the wrong you did to me!"
Wait for the LORD, and he will save you.

Proverbs 20:22, NIrV

*W*hen you find yourself in a situation where you are being treated badly by someone, talk to God about it. Then release your frustration and ask Him to help you find positive ways to deal with your situation. Be sure to treat everyone, regardless of how that person has treated you, with respect and fairness. Break the chain of retribution by setting a new positive standard of personal relations that will build bridges rather than fences. Trust that God will work all things together for the highest good of all.

Don't pay back evil with evil. Don't pay back unkind words with
unkind words. Instead, pay them back with kind words.

1 Peter 3:9, NIrV

Revenge, at first though sweet,
bitter erelong back on itself recoils.

JOHN MILTON

TODAY
is the DAY...

To Be an Encourager

May our Lord Jesus Christ Himself and God
our Father . . . comfort and strengthen
your hearts in every good work and word.

2 Thessalonians 2:16–17, NAS

*U*plifting words and actions can be powerful tools in the hand of God. With them, He can encourage a weary soul or bring a wayward heart to repentance. He can restore a life or fulfill a long-forgotten dream. God could do those things without you, but He chooses to use human lips and human hands to deliver comfort and encouragement. In that way, He ensures that *two* people will be strengthened and uplifted—the giver and the receiver. Today is another opportunity to encourage others in word and deed.

We pursue the things which make for peace
and the building up of one another.

Romans 14:19, NAS

Encouragement costs you nothing to give,
but it is priceless to receive.

AUTHOR UNKNOWN

TODAY
is the DAY...

To Be an Example to Others

*Train a child in the way he should go. When
he is old, he will not turn away from it.*

Proverbs 22:6, NIrV

*W*hen it comes to being an example to others, actions really do speak louder than words. Knowing others are watching can open your eyes to choices and habits that could use a little extra prayer and attention. When you are tempted to settle or compromise on your values, think again. It is not just about being good when people can see you. It is also about being great, living up to your God-given potential. If you have heroes who inspire you, remember that you, too, can be a hero who inspires others.

In all things show yourself to be an example of good deeds.

Titus 2:7, NAS

It is easier to exemplify values than teach them.
THEODORE HESBURGH

TODAY
is the DAY...

To Be Honest in Everything

A lying tongue hates those it crushes,
and a flattering mouth works ruin.

Proverbs 26:28, NAS

*T*he words that come out of people's mouths are like plants in a garden. Their speech can be filled with flowers or overgrown with weeds. Habits such as exaggeration, false flattery, or stretching the truth to save face are signals that the heart needs a little yard work. Ask God to help you pull up lies by their dishonest roots. Be honest not only in your words, but in your thoughts and deeds. Practice a deep honesty that is not afraid to admit weakness to God and ask for help.

Buy the truth. Don't sell it. Get wisdom,
training and understanding.

Proverbs 23:23, NIrV

Honesty has a beautiful and refreshing simplicity about it.
No ulterior motives. No hidden meanings. An absence of
hypocrisy, duplicity, political games, and verbal superficiality.

CHARLES R. SWINDOLL

TODAY *is the* DAY...

To Learn from Mistakes

Sometimes it takes a painful experience
to make us change our ways.

Proverbs 20:30, GNT

*M*istakes are the construction zones of life that make you slam on the brakes and ask yourself, "What is going on here?" They are reminders that everyone, no matter how young or old, is a work in progress. A toddler learning to walk is not afraid of falling. A musician practices many hours before he plays a piece perfectly. For God to complete His work in your heart, you have to be willing to risk making mistakes and to learn from them, no matter where you are on life's journey.

Learn prudence; acquire intelligence, you who lack it.

Proverbs 8:5, NRSV

Learn from the mistakes of others—you can't
live long enough to make them all yourself.

MARTIN VANBEE

TODAY
is the DAY...

To Express Yourself

We all have gifts. They differ in keeping with
the grace that God has given each of us.

Romans 12:6, NIrV

*L*ife is a gift, given to you by God. Gifts and talents came
in the package with you at birth. You might have been
attracted to a special interest when you were a child, or
demonstrated an early talent. Now is the time to renew
and cultivate these gifts and talents. God means for every
person to be an expression of His love—so express yourself.
Let yourself love what you love—painting, singing, gardening, building things, helping others. Use your gifts and
talents for the glory of God.

I will sing a new song to You, O God; on a
harp of ten strings I will sing praises to You.

Psalm 144:9, NKJV

We all have many God-given gifts. The challenge with which we are
each faced is to discover these gifts and then make full use of them.

JOHN GRAY

TODAY
is the **DAY...**

TO

Keep a Clear Conscience

·

Work with Resolve

·

Adjust Your Attitude

·

Live with Contentment

·

Grow Strong

·

Be Cheerful

·

Get a Fresh Start

·

Be Contented

·

Cultivate Joy

God did not call us to be successful,
but to be faithful.

MOTHER TERESA

Don't let love and truth ever leave you.

Proverbs 3:3, NIrV

TODAY
is the DAY...

To Do Your Best

The longings of people who work hard are completely satisfied.
Proverbs 13:4, NIrV

*D*iligence is measured by how much of your heart you give to the task at hand. Choosing to give yourself physically, emotionally, and mentally to any job, particularly one that is intense or detailed, takes focus and dependence on the One who enables you to accomplish with excellence whatever task He sets before you. Give the best of yourself to work today. And give the best you can give to your relationships with others and with God. You will be delighted with the final results—a life that is worth living.

The plans of people who work hard succeed.
Proverbs 21:5, NIrV

Few things are impossible to diligence and skill.
SAMUEL JOHNSON

TODAY
is the DAY...

To Keep a Clear Conscience

Keep your faith and a clear conscience.
1 Timothy 1:19, GNT

*W*hat some people call "intuition" or a "sixth sense" can also be your God-driven conscience. It is a personal guidance system that helps you stay away from situations that may not be in your best interest. A clear conscience helps you stay in tune with God and aware of the motivations of your own heart. As your heart becomes more like God's, you want to turn away from anything that has the potential to dishonor Him. Think about the importance of listening to God's still, small voice before you make decisions.

The LORD gave us mind and conscience;
we cannot hide from ourselves.

Proverbs 20:27, GNT

> *Conscience tells us in our innermost being of the presence*
> *of God and of the moral difference between good and evil.*
>
> BILLY GRAHAM

TODAY
is the DAY...
To Use Common Sense

*Folly is a joy to one who has no sense, but a person
of understanding walks straight ahead.*

Proverbs 15:21, NRSV

Sometimes knowing when to step out in faith and when
to use common sense feels like a balancing act. Common
sense is frequently learned through trial and error. The
Book of Proverbs is filled with common sense that otherwise would have to be learned through life's hard knocks.
The advice in Proverbs is simple and direct. You will find
that common sense is the ground from which flights of
faith are launched. First do what common sense dictates.
Then let God tell you when it is time to launch out in faith.

Wise people see danger and go to a safe place.

Proverbs 22:3, NIrV

---

*Faith is believing in things when
common sense tells you not to.*

GEORGE SEATON

TODAY
is the **DAY...**

To Stop Procrastinating

When you make a promise to God,
keep it as quickly as possible.

Ecclesiastes 5:4, GNT

*E*veryone has something in his life that he seems to put off doing. It may be finishing a college degree, buying a house, or applying for a promotion. It may be something simple like painting the house, cleaning the garage, or balancing the checkbook. Ultimately, if some project never gets accomplished, you have no one to blame except yourself. What a waste to look back and say, "If only I had . . ." Make yourself accountable to God to get yourself moving. Take one small step today toward your goal.

A farmer too lazy to plow his fields at the right
time will have nothing to harvest.

Proverbs 20:4, GNT

A lazy person, whatever the talents with which he set out, will have condemned himself to second-hand thoughts and to second-rate friends.

CYRIL CONNOLLY

TODAY
is the DAY...
To Work with Resolve

*Render service with enthusiasm, as to the Lord and not to men
and women, knowing that whatever good we do,
we will receive the same again from the Lord.*

Ephesians 6:7–8, NRSV

*N*o matter what task you find before you, if you are willing to work with your whole heart, you will find blessing
in the midst of what you do. So offer your work to God
and see it as a co-creation with and gift to Him. You will
find satisfaction and delight in even the most mundane
task. Work with focus and resolve, yet with a light heart,
knowing that your work is a way of practicing the presence
of God and creating a blessing for yourself and for others.

*Whatever your task, put yourselves into it,
as done for the Lord.*

Colossians 3:23, NRSV

---

*Hard work is a thrill and a joy when
you are in the will of God.*

ROBERT A. COOK

TODAY
is the DAY...

To Adjust Your Attitude

A cheerful look brings joy to the heart.
Proverbs 15:30, NIV

A cheerful home is a place of welcome for both family and friends. Your attitude is contagious, and your friends and family will pick up on it. Even when circumstances are less than perfect, there is great joy in knowing that God can bring something good out of every situation, big or small. That is the true foundation of a positive attitude. So if you want a cheerful home filled with cheerful hearts, the first attitude check you need to make is on your own.

A cheerful heart makes you healthy.
Proverbs 17:22, NIrV

---

*Wondrous is the strength of cheerfulness,
and its power of endurance.*
THOMAS CARLYLE

TODAY
is the DAY...
To Enjoy Growing Older

Gray hair is a crown of splendor;
it is attained by a righteous life.

Proverbs 16:31, NIV

*I*t is a fact. Every day you wake up, you are older than the day before. But the fact that your body has grown a day older does not mean that you have to grow old inside. There is an eternal spring of youthfulness within your heart, a fountain of life that brings God's wisdom, compassion, and joy to every day. Each morning is an opportunity to wake up and ask God to help you savor this day, this moment in your life. Then you will enjoy a taste of heaven on earth.

Having respect for the LORD leads to a longer life.
Proverbs 10:27, NIrV

To know how to grow old is the master work of wisdom and one
of the most difficult chapters in the great art of living.
HENRI FRÉDÉRIC AMIEL

TODAY
is the DAY...

To Live with Contentment

> *Don't make me either poor or rich, but give me only the*
> *bread I need each day. If you don't, I might have too much.*
> *Then I might say I don't know you. I might say, "Who is*
> *the LORD?" Or I might become poor and steal. Then I*
> *would bring shame to the name of my God.*

Proverbs 30:8-9, NIrV

*C*ontentment and gratitude come with the right perspective. As a citizen of the world's richest country, you are incredibly blessed. Consider this—one-fifth of the world's population (1.2 billion people) live on less than one dollar a day in conditions of almost unimaginable suffering and want. Be grateful for the simple blessings you enjoy. Savor the simple things that make life worth living, and remember to share your surplus with others. Then you will find the heart of true contentment.

> *Better is a little with the fear of the LORD,*
> *than great treasure with trouble.*

Proverbs 15:16, NKJV

True contentment is a real, even an active virtue—not only affirmative but creative It is the power of getting out of any situation all there is in it.

G. K. CHESTERTON

TODAY
is the DAY...
To Guard Your Health

Have respect for the LORD and avoid evil. That will bring health to your body. It will make your bones strong.

Proverbs 3:7–8, NIrV

*G*od has given you a wonderful body. Your body is a marvel that digests food and turns it into fuel for thinking and doing. While you may not understand how the body works, you know what makes it stop working. Here is a simple formula for a happy life: maintain a healthy balance. Give proper attention to each vital area, including relationships, finances, spiritual growth, and physical health. Take care of the body God gave you so you can live a balanced life. Vital health helps you live life more fully.

Beloved, I pray that all may go well with you and that you may be in good health.

3 John 2, NRSV

Look at your health; and if you have it praise God, and value it next to a good conscience.

IZAAK WALTON

TODAY
is the DAY...

To Grow Strong

*You will receive the strength you need
when you stay calm and trust in me.*

Isaiah 30:15, NIrV

*H*uman stamina at times simply cannot keep you going in tough times. When you are tempted to quit, choose instead the strength of faith in God. Cultivate strength of character. Meditate on the Bible and remind yourself that you are not alone in this time of trial. The things that God has laid on your heart to do are important to Him, too, and He will back your strength with His when your endurance comes up short. Ask God to give you His strength today to carry out His will.

I can do all things through Christ who strengthens me.

Philippians 4:13, NKJV

---

*Nothing is so strong as gentleness: nothing
so gentle as real strength.*

SAINT FRANCIS DE SALES

TODAY
is the DAY...
To Be Cheerful

A cheerful heart has a continual feast.
Proverbs 15:15, NAS

*H*ere is a little secret: cheerfulness is a choice. No matter what happens to you, you can choose how to react to it. Even the worst life experience can be met with a positive attitude and a determination to find the good that God can bring from it. When you choose a cheerful attitude, you create a space for God to work miracles. As God was creating the world, He pronounced each day, without exception, as good. You can do the same with each day of your life and choose cheerfulness.

A cheerful heart makes you healthy.
But a broken spirit dries you up.
Proverbs 17:22, NIrV

Everyone must have felt that a cheerful friend is like a sunny day,
which sheds its brightness on all around.
AUTHOR UNKNOWN

TODAY *is the* DAY...

To Protect Yourself

*He provides help and protection for those who are righteous
and honest. He protects those who treat others fairly,
and guards those who are devoted to him.*

Proverbs 2:7–8, GNT

*W*hen you were young, your parents protected you from harm. They kept knives out of your reach, made sure your seat belt was buckled, and kept your vaccinations up to date. You need to be as wise about protecting yourself. Make sure your affairs are in order and take commonsense precautions. Surround yourself with trustworthy people. But remember, too, that God is your true protection. Then you can live with a light heart, knowing you have done your best and that God will do the rest.

*The LORD is my rock and my fortress and my deliverer; the
God of my strength, in whom I will trust; my shield . . . my
stronghold and my refuge; my Savior.*

2 Samuel 22:2–3, NKJV

---

*God is the protector of the believers; he brings
them forth from the shadows into the light.*

KÄTHE KOLLWITZ

TODAY
is the DAY...
To Calm Down

The LORD is a refuge for the oppressed,
a stronghold in times of trouble.

Psalm 9:9, NIV

*W*hen you are tossed by tempests of trouble and stress,
God's presence provides a peaceful oasis in the midst of
chaos. The key is to take your eyes off the storm and to put
them directly on Him. When tension is running high,
make it a point to find a quiet spot where you will not be
disturbed and take a moment to sit quietly with God, asking for His peace and perspective. God has the power to
calm the storms that surround you as well as the ones
brewing within.

O LORD, be gracious to us; we long for you. Be our strength
every morning, our salvation in time of distress.

Isaiah 33:2, NIV

Anxiety comes from strain and strain is caused by too complete a
dependence on ourselves, on our own devices, our own plans,
our own idea of what we are able to do.

THOMAS MERTON

TODAY
is the DAY...

To Get Enough Sleep

When you lie down, you will sleep soundly.
Proverbs 3:24, NIrV

$\int$ leep is a gift, given by the very One who created your need for it. While our fast-paced society rewards workaholics who push the body beyond its limits, the godly person honors the body's need for rest and renewal. If you find yourself tossing and turning, turn to the God who never sleeps. Hand over every care that is weighing heavy on your mind. Let the natural process of a good night's sleep bring you renewed perspective in the morning. Let life's rhythm of rest cradle you in God's love.

In vain you rise early and stay up late, toiling for food to eat—for he grants sleep to those he loves.
Psalm 127:2, NIV

---

*Thank God for sleep! And when you cannot sleep,
still thank Him that you live to lie awake.*
JOHN OXENHAM

TODAY
is the DAY...
To Get a Fresh Start

Those who erase a sin by forgiving it show love. But those who talk about it come between close friends.

Proverbs 17:9, NIrV

*T*hink about yesterday. What is one thing that really made you mad? Weigh the value of holding on to that frustration—will it change the outcome? You could focus on the problem, get mad, build up a grudge, and then tell others what happened. Or you can let go of ill feelings when things go wrong. The choice is yours. You can dwell in the problems of the past or you can move on and enjoy today's experiences and blessings. Thank God for the forgiveness that gives everyone a fresh start.

Forgive us the wrongs we have done, as we forgive the wrongs that others have done to us.

Matthew 6:12, GNT

Forgiveness ought to be like a canceled note—torn in two and burned up so that it never can be shown against one.

HENRY WARD BEECHER

TODAY
is the DAY...
To Honor Your Body

I praise you, for I am fearfully and wonderfully made.
Wonderful are your works; that I know very well.

Psalm 139:14, NRSV

Your body is a gift from a loving God. However, it is a gift that requires attention and care. Making wise choices about the fuel you put into it, the rest and exercise you give it, and the regular checkups you schedule for it are ways of saying thank you to God. Honor the body as well for its complexity and wonder. You are fearfully and wonderfully made, so notice how rich life is because you have senses to experience life and a body to express your gratitude to God.

[God's words] are life to those who find them.
They are health to your whole body.

Proverbs 4:22, NIrV

Look to your health; and if you have it, praise God,
and value it next to a good conscience.

IZAAK WALTON

TODAY
is the DAY...

To Be Contented

*Bless the LORD, O my soul,
and forget not all His benefits.*

Psalm 103:2, NKJV

*C*ontentment is rare in a consumer society. But in all the buying and selling, you lose sight of the fact that you are beloved in the eyes of God, just as you are. Look around you and see that you already have what you need to enjoy the gift of contentment. You have health, you have enough for today, and you have many blessings to count. Just for today, be contented with what you have. Make a choice to rejoice in the riches God has already bestowed on you.

*Be content with such things as you have. For He Himself has
said, "I will never leave you nor forsake you."*

Hebrews 13:5, NKJV

---

*He who is not contented with little
will never be satisfied with much.*

THOMAS BENTON BROOKS

TODAY
is the DAY...
To Take Time Off

You show me the path of life. In your presence there is fullness of joy; in your right hand are pleasures forevermore.

Psalm 16:11, NRSV

*G*enesis records that God rested on the seventh day after creating the world. A Sabbath day was ordained for God's people as a day of rest. In a 24-7 world, it is tempting to just keep multitasking and to never stop to rest. But human beings are not machines. Time for rest, relaxation, and renewal is needed. Take some time away today to enjoy the moment, whether it is taking a lunch break a little longer than usual or declaring a day off to soothe your soul and clear your mind.

*Oh, taste and see that the LORD is good;
blessed is the man who trusts in Him!*

Psalm 34:8, NKJV

---

*It is the heart that is not yet sure of its God
that is afraid to laugh in His presence.*

GEORGE MACDONALD

TODAY *is the* DAY...

TO

Laugh More Often

·

Free Your Mind

·

Expect Joy

·

Start Talking to God

·

Trust God's Timing

·

Give Your Dreams to God

·

Acknowledge God Is in Control

·

Allow God to Lead

·

Rest in God's Safety

Anxiety does not empty tomorrow of its sorrows,
but only empties today of its strength.
CHARLES HADDON SPURGEON

The lips of the righteous nourish many.
Proverbs 10:21, NIV

TODAY
is the DAY...
To Know Yourself

It is your own face that you see reflected in the water and it is your own self that you see in your heart.

Proverbs 27:19, GNT

The attitudes and values in your heart are expressed each day on your face, in your voice, and through your actions. While outside circumstances do influence you, who you are is clearly demonstrated in the way you handle everyday situations. Prayer and self-examination help you know yourself and keep your motivations pure. As you cultivate a relationship with God, He will live in your heart. Others can see when God is living on the inside of your heart. His Spirit gives you peace and joy even in challenging situations.

> *He that respects himself is safe from others;*
> *he wears a coat of mail that none can pierce.*
> HENRY WADSWORTH LONGFELLOW

TODAY
is the DAY...

To Cultivate Joy

Those who sow in tears shall reap in joy.
Psalm 126:5, NKJV

*K*eep in mind that God is your source of joy. Joy is a natural expression of the life of faith, and it needs to be cultivated. Start by being thankful for this moment and all it offers. Even if the circumstances are difficult and you feel that happiness is elusive, God promises joy even in sorrow. Cultivate your relationship with God, and you will be cultivating the seeds of joy. If you are willing to invest time and energy in helping others, you will discover that loving service fills your heart with quiet joy.

*The kingdom of God is not eating and drinking, but
righteousness and peace and joy in the Holy Spirit.*

Romans 14:17, NKJV

*Christ is not only a remedy for your weariness and trouble,
but he will give you an abundance of the contrary, joy and delight.*
JONATHAN EDWARDS

TODAY *is the* **DAY...**

To Laugh More Often

A merry heart makes a cheerful countenance.
Proverbs 15:13, NKJV

*R*esearchers say that laughing is great for your health. It reduces stress and increases your tolerance to pain and releases infection-fighting antibodies. What is more, humor increases your attentiveness, your heart rate, and even your energy level. Laughter really is the best medicine. It is also good for lightening your mood, helping you gain a fresh perspective on life, and helping you remember that there is more to life than being busy and important. Look on the funny side of things. You will not only be happier, but you will also be a lot more fun to be around.

He will fill your mouth with laughter.
Shouts of joy will come from your lips.
Job 8:21, NIrV

> *Give me a keen and ever present sense of humor; it is the next best thing to an abiding faith in providence.*
> GEORGE B. CHEEVER

TODAY *is the* DAY...

To Free Your Mind

Anxiety weighs down the human heart,
but a good word cheers it up.

Proverbs 12:25, NRSV

*A*nxiety does not solve any problems. It just hangs there in the background of your life, sapping will and energy that could be used for better purposes. When anxiety is dragging you down, lift your eyes to God. Ask for His wisdom to help free your mind from the petty worries that drain and distort. Make a moment-by-moment decision to look past the difficulties in your situation and free your mind of worry and anxiety. As you release yourself into God's care, He will fill you with His peace.

Do not be afraid of sudden fear nor of the onslaught of the
wicked when it comes; for the LORD will be your confidence
and will keep your foot from being caught.

Proverbs 3:25–26, NAS

Anxiety does not empty tomorrow of its sorrow,
but only empties today of its strength.

CHARLES HADDON SPURGEON

TODAY
is the DAY...
To Expect Joy

Those who do right can expect joy.
Proverbs 10:28, NIrV

*J*oy is waiting to be cultivated in your life. If you expect joy, you will find it. You will create the circumstances that make life joyous. Start by finding joy in the small blessings that life brings: a child's smile, a flower, sunshine. Then find joy in work well done. Enjoy the pile of clean laundry, the finished report, the meal cooked, and the desk set in order. Find quiet joy in being in God's presence, having a quiet moment alone with Him. If you look for joy, you will find it.

You have made known to me the path of life; [O Lord,]
you will fill me with joy in your presence,
with eternal pleasures at your right hand.

Psalm 16:11, NIV

Real joy comes not from ease or riches or from the
praise of men, but from doing something worthwhile.
PIERRE CONEILLE

TODAY
is the DAY...
To Be Well

Present your bodies as a living sacrifice, holy and
acceptable to God, which is your spiritual worship.

Romans 12:1, NRSV

*G*od wants you to be completely well so that He can accomplish all that He has planned to do in and through you. Do your part to keep yourself in good health physically, mentally, and spiritually. If you have health issues, pray for guidance as you explore new options. Be open to new natural treatments as well as traditional medicine. Let God show you what can be accomplished when the two of you work together toward a goal of total wellness. Consider it a way of honoring your Creator.

You have been bought with a price:
therefore glorify God in your body.

1 Corinthians 6:20, NAS

Take care of your health, that it may serve you to serve God.
SAINT FRANCIS DE SALES

TODAY
is the DAY...
To Start Talking to God

The LORD is far from the wicked but
he hears the prayer of the righteous.

Proverbs 15:29, NIV

*I*f you have been neglecting your prayer life, you have been neglecting a lifeline. It is time to start talking to God again. He is there to listen to your troubles, to guide you through perilous times, and to rejoice with you when you are happy. Spending time in prayer with God is the best investment you can make. It will pay dividends of peace, wisdom, and joy. A loving relationship with God makes each day precious. He loves to listen. He loves to answer. Why not start talking to God right now?

Devote yourselves to prayer.

Colossians 4:2, NIV

> *Heaven is full of answers to prayer for*
> *which no one ever bothered to ask.*
> BILLY GRAHAM

TODAY *is the* DAY...

To Follow God's Direction

In all your ways acknowledge Him,
and He shall direct your paths.

Proverbs 3:6, NKJV

*I*t would be great if life came with a detailed set of directions. But no set of rules can replace the personal guidance of a vital relationship with God. God wants you to grow close to Him and to develop faith in Him to provide direction for your life. He does not simply sit up in heaven and issue antiseptic directions, either. He is with you in each decision. He created you, He knows you, He loves you—and He will never steer you wrong! Is God directing your journey?

I guide you in the way of wisdom. I lead you along straight
paths. When you walk, nothing will slow you down.
When you run, you won't trip and fall.

Proverbs 4:11–12, NIrV

If God sends us on stony paths,
he provides strong shoes.

CORRIE TEN BOOM

TODAY
is the DAY...
To Trust God's Timing

*You, LORD, give perfect peace to those who keep
their purpose firm and put their trust in you.*

Isaiah 26:3, GNT

*L*ife has many unexpected setbacks and delays. It can be frustrating. It is likely that you are the one who gets the most impatient with your progress. But there is more than meets the eye. While you are being impatient with the lack of progress, this delay may be an important lesson, or a mercy of God's timing preventing you from even greater obstacles and problems. Trust God and be patient with the process. There is power in patience as you learn to wait on God's perfect timing.

*If we hope for what we do not yet have,
we wait for it patiently.*

Romans 8:25, NIV

---

*Be patient with everyone,
but above all with yourself.*
SAINT FRANCIS DE SALES

TODAY
is the DAY...
To Obey God

*Obey the LORD, be humble, and you will
get riches, honor, and a long life.*

Proverbs 22:4, GNT

*O*bedience to God is not a slavish following of a set of
rules for good behavior. Obeying God is more like walking
in step with a friend and going in the same direction
together. Walking along the path with God is more
rewarding than straying off on your own. Have confidence
that obedience will take you to the right place where God
intends for you to be. Live by kingdom priorities. God
always knows what is best for you. Obey Him and you will
always be able to find your way!

*If you love me, you will
obey what I command.*

John 14:15, NIV

---

*Obedience to God is always
for our good and His glory.*

AUTHOR UNKNOWN

TODAY *is the* DAY...

To Come Clean Before God

Human wisdom, brilliance, insight—they are
of no help if the LORD is against you.

Proverbs 21:30, GNT

*G*od loves you, and He wants you to grow and thrive
spiritually. That can happen if you are willing to open your
heart completely and honestly to Him. He can clean your
life by seeking out and sweeping away even the tiniest
traces of sin. If you cannot be honest before God, how will
you ever be honest with yourself? Even when you do not
understand the work He is doing, set your human insights
aside. Trust God as His cleansing fire brings a new growth
of holiness into your life.

Sometimes it takes a painful experience
to make us change our ways.

Proverbs 20:30, GNT

Holiness does not consist in doing uncommon things,
but in doing every thing with purity of heart.
CARDINAL HENRY E. MANNING

TODAY
is the DAY...

To Give Your Dreams to God

The human mind may devise many plans, but it is the purpose of the LORD that will be established.

Proverbs 19:21, NRSV

You have dreams for your life; we all do. Relinquishing your dreams to God is the strongest test of faith you will ever face. But it is a test you must pass if you are to become all you were meant to be, all God created you to be. By releasing your grip on the control of your life, you free God to work miracles and direct you onto the path of true success. As you ask, give God the opportunity to give you what you want—or something better.

"My thoughts are not your thoughts, neither are your ways my ways," declares the LORD. "As the heavens are higher than the earth, so are my ways higher than your ways and my thoughts than your thoughts."

Isaiah 55:8–9, NIV

Not as I will, but as thou wilt. To be able to say these words and truly mean them is the highest point we can ever hope to attain.

MALCOLM MUGGERIDGE

TODAY
is the **DAY...**

To Set Your Mind on God

The LORD detests the thoughts of the wicked,
but those of the pure are pleasing to him.

Proverbs 15:26, NIV

*I*t is easy for a train of thought to jump the tracks and career downhill. It is important to guard what goes into your mind and what you spend time meditating on. Prayer and meditation help you focus on higher things. You can learn to see life from God's perspective if you will learn to know the mind of God. Ask God for wisdom. Even if your actions are well intentioned, if your thoughts are contrary to God's design, you will miss out on the peace, joy, and contentment He has planned for you.

A tranquil mind gives life to the flesh.

Proverbs 14:30, NRSV

To think well is to serve God in the interior court:
To have a mind composed of divine thoughts, to be like him within.

THOMAS TRAHERNE

TODAY
is the DAY...

To Emulate God's Character

Those who guard their way preserve their lives.
Proverbs 16:17, NRSV

*T*he purpose of camouflage is to blend in with your surroundings. Succumbing to peer pressure is one way of doing just that. This kind of camouflage is not always beneficial, for either kids or adults. Acting like those around you eventually will no longer be an act. It will become a habit. You are called to a higher standard—God's standard. The more you emulate God's character, the more you will be able to stand out in a crowd and be secure in the person God has created you to be.

Don't live any longer the way this world lives. Let your way of thinking be completely changed.

Romans 12:2, NIrV

When you have to make a choice and don't make it, that in itself is a choice.

WILLIAM JAMES

TODAY is the DAY...

To Agree God Is in Control

You will walk on your way securely and your foot will not stumble. If you sit down, you will not be afraid.

Proverbs 3:23–24, NRSV

*L*ife is filled with circumstances that can incite fear in the most courageous of hearts. Learning to "fear not" is more than a matter of keeping a stiff upper lip or living in denial. You cannot control your circumstances, but you can choose your response to circumstances. It is a matter of trusting that the God who loves you will never leave your side. You are to give your fears to God, to surrender to His tender mercies. Embrace the knowledge that He is in control and promises to bring good out of every circumstance.

It is the LORD who goes before you. He will be with you; he will not fail you or forsake you. Do not fear or be dismayed.

Deuteronomy 31:8, NRSV

> *There is never a fear that has not a corresponding "Fear not."*
> AMY WILSON CARMICHAEL

TODAY *is the* DAY...

To Allow God to Lead

The human mind plans the way,
but the LORD directs the steps.

Proverbs 16:9, NRSV

*W*hen God created each one of us, He gave each of us free will. That means our lives are filled with choices. Some choices are almost inconsequential: paper or plastic? Others are life-altering: Whom will you marry? What career path will you follow? When you need to make a decision, ask God to show you the next step. Life often unfolds one step at a time. Instead of rushing ahead like an impatient child, slow down and let God be your guide and show the way, one step at a time.

I guide you in the way of wisdom.
I lead you along straight paths.

Proverbs 4:11, NIrV

> *It is morally impossible to exercise trust in God while there is*
> *failure to wait upon Him for guidance and direction.*
>
> D. E. HOSTE

TODAY
is the DAY...
To Accept God's Comfort

The name of the LORD is a strong tower;
the righteous runs into it and is safe.

Proverbs 18:10, NAS

*I*n the Psalms, God says He holds every one of your tears in a bottle. That means your heart cannot break without affecting God. He cares about your pain, both physical and emotional, and offers His comfort any time of day or night. When life is difficult, be gentle on yourself. Read comforting Bible promises, pray, and allow God to comfort you. Let tears flow. Remember, too, that the words of a friend, a nourishing meal, and a time of rest are practical, tangible gifts of comfort from God.

Praise be to the God and Father of our Lord Jesus Christ,
the Father of compassion and the God of all comfort,
who comforts us in all our troubles.

2 Corinthians 1:3-4, NIV

> *To need consolation and to console are human,*
> *just as human as Christ was.*
>
> DOROTHY SOELLE

TODAY
is the DAY...
To Know God Better

Trust in the LORD with all your heart and lean not on your own understanding; in all your ways acknowledge him, and he will make your paths straight.

Proverbs 3:5–6, NIV

*T*here are many ways to get to know God. Gratitude opens your eyes to see how He blesses you. Prayer is a conversation with Him. Here is another way to get to know God better: as you read through the Bible, personalize it. Whenever God gives a promise, such as "I will never leave you or forsake you," substitute your name for the word *you*. This will bring you face-to-face with God's character and draw a picture of the depth of His love and boundless limits of His power.

Draw near to God, and he will draw near to you. Cleanse your hands, you sinners, and purify your hearts, you double-minded.

James 4:8, NRSV

There is a God-shaped vacuum in the heart of every man which cannot be filled by any created thing, but only by God, the Creator, made known through Jesus.

BLAISE PASCAL

TODAY
is the DAY...

TO

Partner with God

·

Commit Problems to God

·

Thank God for Second Chances

·

Listen to Your Parents

·

Replace Pride with Love

·

Practice Contentment

·

Learn from Others

·

Keep the Facts Straight

·

Learn Something New

As long as you live,
keep learning how to live.

SENECA

Listen to counsel and accept discipline,
that you may be wise the rest of your days.

Proverbs 19:20, NAS

TODAY
is the DAY...
To Rest in God's Safety

He who fears the LORD has a secure fortress,
and for his children it will be a refuge.

Proverbs 14:26, NIV

*G*od is looking out for you, even when you are not aware
of it. You may never know all the ways in which He protects you. In the Bible, He says that He commands His
angels to guard you in all your ways (Psalm 91:11). What a
marvelous promise. Thank God for His protective hand
on your life. When you find yourself in difficult, demand-
ing, or dangerous situations, remember that God is always
with you, and when you know you are safe in His care, you
can rest with calm assurance.

The LORD is my protector; he is my strong fortress.
My God is my protection, and with him I am safe.

Psalm 18:2, GNT

We sleep in peace in the arms of God,
when we yield ourselves up to his Providence.

FRANÇOIS FÉNELON

TODAY *is the* DAY...

To Partner with God

You have started living a new life. It is being made new so that what you know has the Creator's likeness.

Colossians 3:10, NIrV

*W*hen God created humanity, He made us in His image. He is the Creator, and we are creators, too. So consciously choose to be a partner and co-creator with God. God is infinitely more farsighted than you are, and He knows all things. He knows what will work out and what will not. Even when you can accomplish something on your own, enlisting God as your partner will make the process go more smoothly. Do not hesitate to include God in your plans, and trust Him to provide for a successful outcome.

Unless the LORD builds the house, they labor in vain who build it.

Psalm 127:1, NAS

Trust in God does not supersede the employment of prudent means on our part.

PASQUIER QUESNEL

TODAY
is the DAY...
To Be God's Child

Rest in the LORD and wait patiently for Him.
Psalm 37:7, NAS

*I*t is easy to forget that we are all God's children. We try so hard to be adult and in control. God understands and asks us to trust Him instead. So let go of trying to control everything, and rest in the love of God. Pray with a child-like faith. Every time you look in the mirror, remind yourself of your relationship with God and that you are the child of your Father in heaven. You can be confident in asking Him for help when you need it.

How much more will your Father in heaven
give good gifts to those who ask him!
Matthew 7:11, NIV

Prayer is ordained to this end that we should confess our needs to God, and bare our hearts to him, as children lay their troubles in full confidence before their parents.
JOHN CALVIN

TODAY
is the DAY...

To Commit Problems to God

The LORD is my strength and my shield; my heart trusted in Him, and I am helped; therefore my heart greatly rejoices, and with my song I will praise Him.

Psalm 28:7, NKJV

*G*od never intended for you to be controlled by the problems in your life. That is why He took so much care to let you know that you can place your trust in Him. He is the One who cares for you. He does not promise that things will necessarily turn out as you expect them to. But He does say with certainty that He will take care of you in every situation you encounter. You will not have to face the problems of your life alone. God will be there to see you through.

Happy are those who trust in the LORD.

Proverbs 16:20, NRSV

He who trusts in himself is lost.
He who trusts in God can do all things.

SAINT ALPHONSUS LIGUORI

TODAY *is the* DAY...

To Be Glad for New Chances

The merciful man does himself good, but the
cruel man does himself harm.

Proverbs 11:17, NAS

*S*erious mistakes and failures to do things right stem from
not being careful or concerned enough. Thank God that
He does not throw the towel in on anyone. Thank God for
mercy and for second chances! If you have ever failed at
something important and have been given another opportunity to do things right, you probably learned to be thankful for second chances. Learn from your mistakes and
make the most of a new opportunity. And remember to be
willing to give others a second chance, too.

The LORD is longsuffering and abundant in mercy,
forgiving iniquity and transgression.

Numbers 14:18, NKJV

He that has tasted the bitterness of sin fears to commit it; and he
that hath felt the sweetness of mercy will fear to offend it.

WILLIAM COWPER

TODAY
is the DAY...

To Please God

The upright enjoy God's favor.
Proverbs 14:9, NRSV

*W*alking close to God, loving Him, and obeying Him please God and will, over time, transform your life. As your commitment to godly character grows, God's Spirit motivates you to deal honestly, considerately, and fairly with others. Jesus said that the first commandment was to love God wholeheartedly, and that the second was to love your neighbor as yourself. Make choices based upon sincere love for God and others, and consistently choose what is right. This is the kind of faith that pleases God by being honorable.

The boy Samuel was growing in stature
and in favor both with the LORD and with men.

1 Samuel 2:26, NAS

The best characters are made by vigorous
and persistent resistance to evil tendencies.

TIMOTHY DEXTER

TODAY
is the DAY...

To Listen to Your Parents

Listen to your father; without him you would not exist.
When your mother is old, show her your appreciation.

Proverbs 23:22, GNT

*I*t is a truth you know in your heart. When you were a
child you thought your parents knew everything. When
you were an adolescent, you thought they knew nothing.
By the time you became an adult, you probably realized
just how much wisdom your parents accumulated over the
years. It is a wise child who understands that the perspec-
tives of others offer valuable guidance. Your parents are a
source of great insight and common sense. Take the time
to tap into it. Ask them to share their wisdom with you.

Keep your father's commands and do not
forsake your mother's teaching.

Proverbs 6:20, NIV

> *The relationship of parent and child remains indelible and*
> *indestructible, the strongest relationship on earth.*
> THEODOR REIK

TODAY
is the DAY...

To Be There When It Matters

*Two are better than one....If either of them falls, the one
will lift up his companion. But woe to the one who falls
when there is not another to lift him up.*

Ecclesiastes 4:9–10, NAS

*O*ne of God's greatest gifts is the opportunity to have relationships with others. Sometimes relationships carry a serious responsibility. Those with whom you share a relationship depend on you. That means you stay true to your commitments, even though the going may get tough or you simply may not feel like it. What you sow, you reap. The quality of the love you give will be the quality of the love you receive. You will never regret that you were able to be there in a loved one's time of need.

The faithful will abound with blessings.

Proverbs 28:20, NRSV

*Nothing is more noble,
nothing more venerable than fidelity.*
CICERO

TODAY
is the DAY...
To Replace Pride with Love

*Arrogance will bring your downfall, but if
you are humble, you will be respected.*

Proverbs 29:23, GNT

*P*ride seldom uses its own name. If it did, you could easily
spot it and put an end to its destructive ways. Instead, it is
a chameleon, at times portraying itself as love, courage,
success, and other positive character traits. Pride whispers
in your ear that your actions are selfless, your intentions
pure, and your goal beneficent. Beat pride at its own game
by embracing humility, its equal and opposite force. Ask
God to show you where false pride lurks, and replace it
with a humble heart of loving service.

*When pride comes, then comes disgrace,
but with humility comes wisdom.*

Proverbs 11:2, NIV

---

*Pride is the cold mountain peak, sterile and bleak; humility is the
quiet valley fertile and abounding in life, and peace lives there.*

ANN AUSTIN

TODAY
is the DAY...

To Practice Contentment

*Having respect for the LORD leads to life. Then you
will be content and free from trouble.*

Proverbs 19:23, NIrV

*L*iving in a land of plenty, where wants often masquerade
as needs, it can be puzzling to know how much is truly
enough. Contentment is an attitude that can be cultivated.
Instead of responding to the pushy voices of con-
sumerism, turn to the quiet wisdom of God's ways. Find
joy in the small things of life—water flowing from a faucet,
a flower blooming, a child's smile, the wind in the trees.
Give thanks to God for what you have been given, and be
content in His loving presence.

*Such is the end of all who are greedy for gain;
it takes away the life of its possessors.*

Proverbs 1:19, NRSV

---

*It is so important not to waste what is precious
by spending all one's time and emotion on fretting
or complaining over what one does not have.*

EDITH SCHAEFFER

TODAY
is the DAY...
To Learn from Others

Let your ears listen to wisdom.
Apply your heart to understanding.

Proverbs 2:2 NIrV

*L*ife is not an exact science. There are no guarantees that what you do will produce the results you hope and pray for. Learning from other people who have walked more than a mile in your shoes can give you needed strength and direction for the journey. Good friends who know you well can advise you, but you can also learn from others. Interview people you admire for information, asking how they meet the challenges of life. Enrich your understanding through books and studying the Bible, as well.

Without counsel, plans go wrong,
but with many advisers they succeed.

Proverbs 15:22, NRSV

Advice is like snow; the softer it falls, the longer it dwells upon,
and the deeper it sinks into the mind.

SAMUEL TAYLOR COLERIDGE

TODAY
is the DAY...

To Learn Money Management

Those who trust in their riches will wither,
but the righteous will flourish like green leaves.

Proverbs 11:28, NRSV

*M*anaging money can be daunting for people of all ages, and that is an excellent reason for learning financial responsibility early in life. But it is never too late to learn. Living within your means is a learned skill and, at the same time, a responsibility. It takes prayer, planning, and self-control to make money last from one period to the next. Learn to budget your money, spend wisely, give thoughtfully, and save for the future. Learn to see God as your source of good. Trust Him to meet your needs generously.

Why do you spend money for what is not bread,
and your wages for what does not satisfy?

Isaiah 55:2, NAS

There is no wrong with people possessing riches.
The wrong comes when riches possess people.

BILLY GRAHAM

TODAY
is the DAY...

To Respect the Rules

Even children make themselves known by their acts,
by whether what they do is pure and right.

Proverbs 20:11, NRSV

*N*ot all rules are easy to follow. They may even feel constraining, unfair, or downright unnecessary at times. But following rules makes life easier, especially when you do so with a willing spirit. When it comes to knowing right and wrong, we all need to remember the purpose of rules and laws and how they contribute to a civilized, God-honoring society. Whether the rules are traffic laws, family curfews, or the Ten Commandments, their aim is the same—to create a safe space to live a creative and meaningful life.

In the way of righteousness is life,
and in its pathway there is no death.

Proverbs 12:28, NKJV

Whereas obedience is righteousness in relation to God,
love is righteousness in relation to others.

A. PLUMMER

TODAY
is the DAY...

To Keep the Facts Straight

*No one who gossips can be trusted with a secret, but you
can put confidence in someone who is trustworthy.*

Proverbs 11:13, GNT

*K*eeping communication positive means that you are able
to discern the difference between solving a problem and
spreading gossip. That discernment begins by asking God
for wisdom. It continues by sharing your concerns only
with those who are part of the problem or part of the solution—and making absolutely certain you have your facts
straight. Be meticulous in your conversation, and with-
hold judgment till all the facts are in. Then you are free to
share words of hope and healing, becoming one who helps
solve problems instead of making them worse.

*Do you love life and want to see many good days? Then keep your
tongues from speaking evil. Then keep your lips from telling lies.*

Psalm 34:12–13, NIrV

---

*Do not listen gleefully to gossip at your neighbor's expense
or chatter to a person who likes to find fault.*

SAINT MAXIMUS THE CONFESSOR

TODAY
is the DAY...

To Learn Something New

Let wise people listen and add to what they have learned.
Proverbs 1:5, NIrV

*C*hildren are always open and curious, wanting to learn new things. Jesus recommended that His followers be like little children, and you can find childlike joy in learning something new. Take a class, read an exciting book, visit a museum, learn a new skill, or try something you have never tried before. Search for greater understanding in everything you encounter instead of assuming you have all the answers. Nurturing your own curiosity can help you retain a sense of wonder while increasing your appetite for a deeper understanding of God.

Apply your heart to instruction,
and your ears to words of knowledge.

Proverbs 23:12, NKJV

Learning makes a man fit company for himself.
THOMAS FULLER

TODAY
is the DAY...

To Lend a Helping Hand

*Don't hold back good from those who are worthy of it.
Don't hold it back when you can help.*

Proverbs 3:27, NIrV

*I*f you want to *have* good neighbors, you have to *be* a good neighbor. Throughout the Bible are scriptures encouraging you to live a life of charity. One way you can do this is to use whatever ability and energy you have to help those around you. Maybe the older woman down the street needs some carpentry work done. Perhaps a local charity could use your help in the soup kitchen. Or maybe charity needs to begin at home, by helping with long-neglected household chores and repairs.

*Anyone who hates his neighbor commits sin. But blessed
is the person who is kind to those in need.*

Proverbs 14:21, NIrV

*Everybody is under obligation to help and support his
neighbor as he would himself like to be helped.*

MARTIN LUTHER

TODAY
is the DAY...

To Offer Unexpected Kindness

A generous man will prosper; he who refreshes others will himself be refreshed.

Proverbs 11:25, NIV

You do not often think of simple kindness as being generous or refreshing—until you are on the receiving side of it. When it is unexpected and unsolicited, you realize an even greater benefit of relief to your complicated life. The next time you notice someone in need, offer your assistance. When you have an opportunity to do the same for someone else, you will be able to sense a true feeling of joy and self-worth because God created you to love His children. Little kindnesses multiply into a life worth living.

The righteous are like a light shining brightly; the wicked are like a lamp flickering out.

Proverbs 13:9, GNT

Every act of kindness and compassion done by any man for his fellow Christian is done by Christ working within him.

JULIAN OF NORWICH

TODAY
is the DAY...

To Be More Generous

Be generous, and you will be prosperous.
Help others, and you will be helped.

Proverbs 11:25, GNT

*T*here are many ways to exercise generosity. You may have more time than money, more belongings than time. Whatever abundance God has blessed you with, share it with others. But most important, be generous in caring. In that way, you will be fulfilling God's desire for each of us— to love and care for those around us. Do not let your heart become a stagnant pond. As God's blessings flow in, open the doors and let them flow out to others. You will find that in giving you become richer.

Give to others, and God will give to you. Indeed, you will
receive a full measure, a generous helping, poured into your
hands—all that you can hold. The measure you use
for others is the one that God will use for you.

Luke 6:38, GNT

You do not have to be rich to be generous. If he has the spirit
of true generosity, a pauper can give like a prince.
CORRINE U. WELLS

TODAY
is the DAY...

TO

Offer Unexpected Kindness

•

Be More Generous

•

Live Free of "Things"

•

Teach Others

•

Embrace Hope

•

Seek Higher Wisdom

•

Teach Others

•

Seek Advice

•

Stay True

The trouble with most of us is that
we would rather be ruined by
praise than saved by criticism.

NORMAN VINCENT PEALE

*Anything you say to the wise
will make them wiser.*

Proverbs 9:9, GNT

TODAY
is the DAY...
To Live Free of "Things"

When you set your eyes on it, it is gone. For wealth certainly makes itself wings like an eagle that flies toward the heavens.

Proverbs 23:5, NAS

*P*eople sometimes have a tendency to get caught up in material things—it may be a car, a house, a golf club, a painting, a camera, or a big-screen HD television. But all these are just "things." They all will break, wear out, go out of style, or otherwise end up in a landfill. They are not eternal. It is not bad to have these; it only becomes a problem when you focus on your things and miss out on what is really important. Money and things are but temporary. What will last forever is your relationship with God.

Store up for yourselves treasures in heaven ... for where your treasure is, there your heart will be also.

Matthew 6:20-21, NAS

Wealth desired for its own sake obstructs the increase of virtue, and large possessions in the hands of selfish men have a bad tendency.

JOHN WOOLMAN

TODAY
is the DAY...

To Embrace Hope

There is surely a future hope for you,
and your hope will not be cut off.

Proverbs 23:18, NIV

*H*ope is the sense of expectation that washes over you as
you spend time with God in prayer. It is the warm feeling
of assurance you feel as you remember God's faithfulness
in the past. It is the way your soul snaps to attention when
someone comes to you with a word of encouragement.
Hope is what sustains you as you wait for your faith to
become substance. Embrace the hope God sends into
your life and let it stimulate your faith that God will meet
all your needs.

Set all your hope on the grace that Jesus Christ
will bring you when he is revealed.

1 Peter 1:13, NRSV

What oxygen is to the lungs,
such is hope for the meaning of life.
HEINRICH EMIL BRUNNER

TODAY
is the DAY...

To Seek Higher Wisdom

*If you have found [wisdom], there is a prospect,
and your hope will not be cut off.*

Proverbs 24:14, NKJV

It is easy to consider only one or a few angles when pondering a problem. Sometimes you have to stretch your mind to consider all facets of a situation. And sometimes these facets may be a new wrinkle in your awareness. Mental habits can sometimes act as mental blinders. Seek a higher wisdom and perspective from God's point of view. Instead of looking at life from the level of the problem, ask God to help you find fresh solutions that create a new paradigm of understanding and creativity.

*To be wise you must first have reverence for the LORD.
If you know the Holy One, you have understanding.*

Proverbs 9:10, GNT

---

*Of all human pursuits the pursuit of wisdom is the most perfect,
the most sublime, the most profitable, the most delightful.*

SAINT THOMAS AQUINAS

TODAY
is the DAY...
To Teach Others

Let the word of Christ dwell in you richly in all wisdom, teaching and admonishing one another in psalms and hymns and spiritual songs, singing with grace in your hearts to the Lord.

Colossians 3:16, NKJV

*Y*ou teach others first by example. Others learn by watching you: who you are, what you say, and the choices you make. But you may be able to teach in other ways as well. Perhaps you have a special skill that you would be willing to share with others. Whether you are teaching bookkeeping or gardening, you are enriching lives with the knowledge and experience you have gained over the years. An even greater gift is to become a mentor to someone who needs the benefit of your wisdom and experience.

Let your speech always be with grace, as though seasoned with salt, so that you will know how you should respond to each person.

Colossians 4:6, NAS

The mediocre teacher tells. The good teacher explains. The superior teacher demonstrates. The great teacher inspires.
WILLIAM A. WARD

TODAY
is the DAY...
To Stay True

Good people will be rewarded for their deeds.
Proverbs 14:14, GNT

*N*one of us are capable of staying faithfully on the path of a godly lifestyle without God's help. Because He is faithful to us, we are able to be faithful to Him. When you face temptations, He is there. When you face discouragement, He is there. When you face hardship, He is there. He is always there providing just what you need to stay true in difficult situations. So do not give up or give in. Trust that God will help you keep going when the going gets tough, no matter how long the distance is or how difficult the terrain.

If we are faithless, he remains faithful—
for he cannot deny himself.

2 Timothy 2:13, NRSV

Faith is not believing God can;
it's believing God will.
LEWIS TIMBERLAKE

TODAY
is the DAY...

To Live in Grace

Cast your burden on the LORD, and He shall sustain you;
He shall never permit the righteous to be moved.

Psalm 55:22, NKJV

*A*nyone who flies on a regular basis runs into the frustration of canceled flights, long delays, and missed connections. Similarly, many incidents happen each day that you cannot control. When that is true, accept things as they are and avoid making them worse. Choose to trust in God's grace instead of the fear and frustration. Whatever occurs, see God's hand in every situation. Believe that His higher purposes can work all things together for good. There is peace even in the midst of trouble when you trust in God's grace.

He who trusts in the LORD will prosper.

Proverbs 28:25, NAS

I have held many things in my hands, and I have lost them all;
but whatever I have placed in God's hands, that I still possess.

MARTIN LUTHER

TODAY
is the DAY...
To Stop the Rumors

You shall not go about as a talebearer among
your people....I am the LORD.

Leviticus 19:16, NKJV

*I*t is a truth in life that if there were no tale-hearers, there would be no tale-bearers. And consider this: gossip, which is often based on insufficient or untrue information, rarely lifts anyone up; instead, it spreads unhappiness and leaves hurt in its wake. God's standard requires truth, honesty, and fair dealings. What you sow, you will reap. So do not join in when others gossip. Whenever you are confronted by a gossip session, think about this twist on the Golden Rule—do unto another as if you *were* the other—then walk away.

Gossip is spread by wicked people; they stir
up trouble and break up friendships.

Proverbs 16:28, GNT

Few are they who manage to dam the rush of water.
Still fewer are they who are able to stem the gossiping tongue.

JOHN CLIMACUS

TODAY
is the DAY...

To Be More Hospitable

*He who is generous will be blessed, for he gives
some of his food to the poor.*

Proverbs 22:9, NAS

*F*irst-class hospitality is more than folding napkins into unusual shapes or learning techniques for a stunning presentation or making the perfect cup of coffee. It is offering the love and compassion of God to others. When you open your home to others, you are opening your heart to those God loves. By practicing hospitality with a generous welcome and warmhearted sharing, you become a blessing to the world, and you create a little piece of heaven on earth. Let God love others through your acts of hospitality and sharing.

*Do not neglect to show hospitality to strangers, for by
this some have entertained angels without knowing it.*

Hebrews 13:2, NAS

---

*What is there more kindly than the
feeling between host and guest?*

AESCHYLUS

TODAY
is the DAY...
To Be Happy for Others

A heart at peace gives life to the body,
but envy rots the bones.

Proverbs 14:30, NIV

*S*ometimes it is easy to feel that everyone else has a better life than you do. But letting those feelings draw you into jealous thoughts will only make you feel worse. Remember that God wants to bless you, as well as those you are tempted to envy. Do not allow yourself to become discontented when you see the good fortune of others. Turn your back on envious thoughts and replace them with prayers of thanksgiving. Trust that God will also give you the desires of your heart, as He has promised.

Where envy and self-seeking exist,
confusion and every evil thing are there.

James 3:16, NKJV

> *Envy takes the joy, happiness,*
> *and contentment out of living.*
> BILLY GRAHAM

TODAY
is the DAY...

To Give Thanks for Friends

Faithful are the wounds of a friend,
but deceitful are the kisses of an enemy.

Proverbs 27:6, NAS

*F*riendship is more than compliments. Cherish those friends who tell you what you *need* to hear rather than just what you want to hear. It might be something as simple as helping you choose the right outfit or as complex as being truthful with you about a relationship or an unhealthy habit. Ask God to help you listen to what your friends say, and be willing to return the favor when your friends need your honesty. Thank God for loyal friends who will tell you the truth in love.

Oil and perfume make the heart glad,
so a man's counsel is sweet to his friend.

Proverbs 27:9, NAS

Only your real friends will tell
you when your face is dirty.
SICILIAN PROVERB

TODAY
is the DAY...
To Seek Advice

Plans fail without good advice.
But they succeed when there are many advisers.

Proverbs 15:22, NIrV

*W*ise advice can come from many sources. The key is being open to receive it. You have probably noticed it is easy to go ahead with your plans without consulting anyone. After all, there is always the chance you might hear something that goes against what you have already made up your mind to do. However, it is good to keep in mind that seeking out and heeding wise advice in the beginning often can prevent trouble later. Good advisers are a gift from God, helping you make better decisions.

Where there is no guidance, a nation falls,
but in an abundance of counselors there is safety.

Proverbs 11:14, NRSV

Discuss your affairs with one who
is wise and who fears God.

THOMAS À KEMPIS

TODAY
is the DAY...

To Listen with Love

The LORD has given us eyes to
see with and ears to listen with.

Proverbs 20:12, GNT

*I*t is easy to forget to listen. But listening with all of your attention is one of the greatest gifts you can ever give another human being. Do not interrupt. Do not think about what you are going to say next. Instead, look into the eyes of the person who is talking to you. Take a deep breath, slow down, concentrate on this moment here and now. Ask God to give you ears to hear what the other person is really saying, so that you can see beyond the surface into the heart.

If one gives answer before hearing, it is folly and shame.

Proverbs 18:13, NRSV

It is the province of knowledge to speak
and it is the privilege of wisdom to listen.
OLIVER WENDELL HOLMES

TODAY
is the DAY...

To Choose Friends Carefully

Godly people are careful about the friends they choose.
Proverbs 12:26, NIrV

*P*eople are influenced by their friends. Choose your friends with care. Avoid whiners and complainers. Spend your time with friends who encourage you, maintain a good attitude, and have a positive outlook on life. Sometimes you will have to walk away from toxic relationships, whether it is the buddy who tempts you to unhealthy ways or someone who is always criticizing you. You want friends who are inspiring to be with; people who love God and who want to live in ways that make the world a better place.

Don't be a friend with anyone who burns with anger. Don't go around with a person who gets angry easily. You might learn his habits. And then you will be trapped by them.
Proverbs 22:24–25, NIrV

A friend is called a guardian of love or, as some would have it, a guardian of the spirit itself.
SAINT AELRED OF RIEVAULX

TODAY
is the DAY...

To Choose the Best

Teach me good judgment and knowledge,
for I believe in your commandments.

Psalm 119:66, NRSV

*W*hat is your motivation?" is a question that actors often ask themselves as they prepare to play a role. It is also a great question to ask yourself as you make choices and set priorities. Along with sincere love, wisdom, and concern, motivators such as fear, pride, shame, and selfishness also play a part in your decisions. Are you attracted to a certain choice because it will add to the quality of your life? It takes faith to choose the best. God can help you discern what is best—and then choose it.

The LORD searches every mind,
and understands every plan and thought.

1 Chronicles 28:9, NRSV

Let him have the key to thy heart
who hath the lock to his own.

SIR THOMAS BROWNE

TODAY
is the DAY...
To Pray from the Heart

Godly people cry out, and the LORD hears them.
He saves them from all of their troubles.

Psalm 34:17, NIrV

*P*rayer is a cry of the heart. Some cries may be painful, yet others are joyous, loving, and full of praise. Regardless of the emotion behind the cry, God is always there, listening to hear what His beloved child has to say. Just as earthly friendships deepen through honest conversation, so also do your relationship and communication with God in intimate, heartfelt prayer. Think of your time alone with God as a heart-to-heart conversation with a Best Friend. Bring your triumphs and troubles to One who loves to listen.

Spend a lot of time in prayer.
Always be watchful and thankful.

Colossians 4:2, NIrV

The purpose of all prayer is to find God's will
and to make that will our prayer.
CATHERINE MARSHALL

TODAY
is the **DAY...**

To Share a Hug

Let love and faithfulness never leave you;
bind them around your neck.

Proverbs 3:3, NIV

*L*ove is an action verb that is expressed whenever you meet the needs of another person. One of those needs is physical touch. Cherishing or comforting another physically is one way of putting flesh on the arms of an invisible God. God has given you the privilege of holding your loved ones and your friends close, hugging and embracing them for Him until He can do the same for them in heaven. Make a habit of surprising someone with a hug for no special reason, just because you care.

Love each other deeply. Honor others more than yourselves.

Romans 12:10, NIrV

> *Affection is responsible for nine-tenths of whatever*
> *solid and durable happiness there is in our lives.*
> C. S. LEWIS

TODAY
is the DAY...

To Love Your Neighbor

Owe no one anything except to love one another,
for he who loves another has fulfilled the law.

Romans 13:8, NKJV

A godly life is one of love in action. Choosing loving actions and attitudes toward those around us is a way to love God in what we do and how we treat others. This kind of love is nonjudgmental, warmhearted, and generous. When you reach out a helping hand, offer a word of encouragement, or help create an atmosphere of community and friendliness, you are creating a little bit of the kingdom of God in your corner of the world. Serve God today by loving your neighbor.

Dear children, don't just talk about love.
Put your love into action. Then it will truly be love.

1 John 3:18, NIrV

The love of God is the first and great commandment.
But love of our neighbor is the means by which we obey it.
SAINT AUGUSTINE

TODAY
is the DAY...

To Encourage Your Best Friend

Say only what will help to build others up and meet their needs. Then what you say will help those who listen.

Ephesians 4:29, NIrV

A smile, a kind word, a helping hand—these are the benefits of real friendships. Each day you have the opportunity to make a practical, positive difference in a dear friend's life. Some people always have something negative to say. They complain if it is raining or if the sun is shining. True friends, however, enjoy being together and find ways to encourage one another. Let friends know you believe in them, and be specific in your encouragement. Make sure your friends know that they can count on you.

Encourage one another and help one another, just as you are now doing.

1 Thessalonians 5:11, GNT

Friends are those rare people who ask how we are and then wait to hear the answer.

ED CUNNINGHAM

TODAY
is the DAY...

TO

Be Happy for Others

·

Seek Advice

·

Listen with Love

·

Offer a Prayer

·

Choose the Best

·

Pray from the Heart

·

Love Your Neighbor

·

Be a Good Person

·

Be Considerate

*Fulfillment of your destiny does not
come in a moment, a month,
or a year, but over a lifetime.*

CASEY TREAT

*Blessed are those who hunger and thirst for
righteousness, for they shall be filled.*

Matthew 5:6, NKJV

TODAY *is the* DAY...

To Support Your Friends

A man cannot be established through wickedness,
but the righteous cannot be uprooted.

Proverbs 12:3, NIV

*I*n the same way as roots support a tree, you need to know you can count on friends to be with you through the good times and the difficult times. The only way this can happen is by demonstrating that same commitment to your friends. But it takes more than just two trees (or friends) holding each other up. It is important to let God intertwine your lives. Look for ways to support and encourage your friends. In the process you will find that God will help you grow closer together.

Jonathan said to David, "Go in peace, for we have sworn
friendship with each other in the name of the LORD."

1 Samuel 20:42, NIV

Beauty, strength, youth, are flowers but fading seen;
duty, faith, love, are roots, and ever green.

GEORGE PEELE

TODAY
is the DAY...

To Be a Good Person

A good man obtains favor from the LORD.
Proverbs 12:2, NKJV

*R*eal goodness is more than just good deeds. The kind of consistent goodness that marks a successful life is the result of an ever-deepening relationship with God. As you surrender yourself to Him, His character begins to dominate your life more and more. What makes up God's character? Galatians 5 says that it consists of the following: love, joy, peace, patience, kindness, generosity, faithfulness, gentleness, and self-control. These are characteristics of strength, not weakness, and permeate your very nature. With God's help, you can live a life of goodness.

The good person out of the good treasure
of the heart produces good.
Luke 6:45, NRSV

Goodness is something so simple: Always live for others,
never to seek one's own advantage.
DAG HAMMARSKJÖLD

TODAY
is the DAY...
To Support Loved Ones

Kinsfolk are born to share adversity.
Proverbs 17:17, NRSV

*P*eople grow closer when troubles are shared, when love is expressed through supportive encouragement. Hard times often offer opportunities to demonstrate to one another what is important in life and what love looks like in action. This is a crucial moment to serve God by serving others. Give cheerfully and generously, help ungrudgingly. Express feelings of sincere love and support, especially during hard times. Those values of helping and generosity will be imprinted deeply in everyone's lives. You will always be thankful you chose to give support when it was needed.

If one falls down, his friend can help him up. . . . Though one may be overpowered, two can defend themselves.
Ecclesiastes 4:10, 12, NIV

A friend should bear his friend's infirmities.
WILLIAM SHAKESPEARE

TODAY
is the DAY...

To Treat Your Best Friend

*Some friends play at friendship but a true
friend sticks closer than one's nearest kin.*

Proverbs 18:24, NRSV

A best friend is the person you want to spend more time
with, and who accepts you as you are, warts and all. That
friend also sticks with you through hard times, and you do
the same for him. Value that kind of friend. Make a point
of investing time and energy in that special friendship.
Today is perfect to treat your best friend to something
special. It could be a card, a meal, or tickets to a special
event. How about a boys' or girls' night out at the local
little theater or softball field? Treat your friend—and yourself—to a good time together.

A friend loves at all times.

Proverbs 17:17, NAS

---

*The firmest friendships have been formed in mutual adversity;
as iron is more strongly united by the fiercest flame.*

CALEB C. COLTON

TODAY
is the DAY...
To Be Considerate

What is desirable in a man is his kindness.
Proverbs 19:22, NAS

*B*eing considerate toward others and doing deeds of kindness usually requires only a small amount of time, and your actions show the motivation of your heart to do good. Thoughtful, meaningful deeds are often simply small, passing gestures throughout the day. Smile at a store clerk. Hold the door for a stranger. Be considerate of others' feelings, too. Understand that a thoughtless comment or selfish action on your part may be more wounding than you realize. Courtesy and consideration make life easier, creating an atmosphere that reflects God's love.

Be kind one to another, tenderhearted,
forgiving one another.

Ephesians 4:32, NKJV

Kind looks, kind words, kind acts, and warm handshakes—
these are secondary means of grace when men are in trouble.
JOHN HALL

TODAY
is the DAY...

To Offer a Prayer

The eyes of the LORD are on the righteous,
and His ears are open to their prayers.

1 Peter 3:12, NKJV

*P*rayer is direct access to God, who transcends time and distance and obstacles. Far more than a life preserver to be used only in times of trouble, it is sweet fellowship for every moment of the day. If you have known prayer only as a religious ritual or a last-ditch solution to a problem, open your heart to God and try talking to Him about the everyday things that happen in your life. Every time you feel like talking, God is listening. Offer a simple prayer and listen to God's answer.

The prayer of the upright is His delight.

Proverbs 15:8, NKJV

> *He who has learned to pray has learned the*
> *greatest secret of a holy and a happy life.*
>
> WILLIAM LAW

TODAY
is the DAY...
To Take a Joy Break

This is the day the LORD has made;
we will rejoice and be glad in it.

Psalm 118:24, NKJV

*T*hough the spiritual life is a momentous and mysterious adventure, it is not always a serious proposition. Jesus wept, but He also laughed and took delight in little children. Sometimes the best thing you can do is take a break from all the business of life you take so seriously, and stop and smell the roses. God created a planet of beauty, light, and life. Take joy in creation—from the laughter of children to the common delight of a delicious meal. Lighten up and take a joy break.

Let the righteous be glad; let them rejoice before God;
yes, let them rejoice exceedingly.

Psalm 68:3, NKJV

> *Humor is the prelude to faith and*
> *laughter is the beginning of prayer.*
> REINHOLD NIEBUHR

TODAY
is the DAY...

To Study the Bible

Those who respect the commandment will be rewarded.
Proverbs 13:13, NRSV

The Bible is a love letter to you and your family and friends from God. It is filled with advice on how to live, and it is overflowing with assurance that you are loved. Set aside a regular time each day to read a section of the Scriptures and meditate on what they mean to you personally. The better you know God and His Word, the more you will find yourself using the Bible as a resource and comfort as you meet the challenges of creating a successful and rewarding life.

The word of God is living and powerful,
and sharper than any two-edged sword.

Hebrews 4:12, NKJV

Spiritual reading is mostly a lover's activity—a dalliance with words,
reading as much between the lines as in the lines themselves.
EUGENE PETERSON

TODAY
is the DAY...
To Allow Yourself to Grieve

Blessed be the God and Father of our Lord Jesus Christ,
the Father of mercies and God of all comfort,
who comforts us in all our affliction.

2 Corinthians 1:3–4, NAS

*W*hen grief touches your life, God is there to comfort you. He is the Word when there are no words, the Healer when it appears all hope is gone. He is with you in your grief. Denying your grief or pushing your feelings down only makes the pain worse. God does not expect you to be superhuman, always upbeat and happy. You do not fail Him because you are sad. God knows and understands your human emotions. Take your tears to Him, for He loves you in times of grief as well as in times of joy.

My flesh and my heart may fail, but God is the
strength of my heart and my portion forever.

Psalm 73:26, NAS

Grief can be your servant, helping you to
feel more compassion for others who hurt.

ROBERT SCHULLER

TODAY
is the DAY...

To Give Thanks

*Blessings are like crowns on the
heads of those who do right.*

Proverbs 10:6, NIrV

Blessings are marks of God's love. And when a loving God pours His fullness into your life, you overflow with blessings. Whether in times of joy or sorrow, prosperity or need, God's blessings are evident. All you need is the ability to see them clearly. A thankful heart serves as the perfect pair of glasses to help you do just that. The more you give thanks, the more you notice how much you have to be thankful for. So give thanks today for what you have received.

*How wonderful are the good things you keep for those
who honor you! Everyone knows how good you are,
how securely you protect those who trust you.*

Psalm 31:19, GNT

---

*Those blessings are sweetest that are won
with prayers and worn with thanks.*

THOMAS GOODWIN

TODAY
is the DAY...

To Pray for Understanding

*The LORD gives wisdom, and from his
mouth come knowledge and understanding.*

Proverbs 2:6, NIV

Jot down a few dilemmas for which you asked God's help
in the past. Think about how the problems or situations
were resolved. When you pray for God's intervention,
know that you cannot presume to know how God will
choose to answer. Earnestly seek God's wisdom, and keep
your mind and heart open to His rescue attempts. Avoid
any preconceived notions that might block your sight of
God's plan. Pray that God will bless you with understanding, and that through this understanding, you can with-
stand the challenges of this world.

*Wisdom is the principal thing; therefore get wisdom.
And in all your getting, get understanding.*

Proverbs 4:7, NKJV

---

*We should spend as much time in thanking God
for his benefits as we do in asking him for them.*

SAINT VINCENT DE PAUL

TODAY
is the DAY...

To Perform Spiritual Upkeep

*Do not forget my teaching, but let
your heart keep my commandments.*

Proverbs 3:1, NAS

*T*he only way to protect a car is to invest time and energy in keeping it maintained. In the same way, if you want to keep a healthy body and spirit, you must care for them daily. When you focus on God's ways, you develop the integrity of your soul. Determine to spend at least ten minutes each day reading your Bible and an additional ten minutes talking and listening to God. Allow God to be your spiritual mechanic—think what a fabulous tune-up that would be!—and you will see the difference in your life.

*How blessed are those who observe His testimonies,
who seek Him with all their heart.*

Psalm 119:2, NAS

---

*A man too busy to take care of his health is like
a mechanic too busy to take care of his tools.*

SPANISH PROVERB

TODAY
is the DAY...
To Quit Lying

Truthful lips endure forever,
but a lying tongue lasts only a moment.

Proverbs 12:19, NIV

*L*isten to yourself. Do you embellish the truth? You only fool yourself if you think others are not aware when you lie. A single lie leads to a second and a third as you continue having to cover your tracks. Often it becomes so complicated that it is impossible to remember whom you have told what, and you finally end up just embarrassing yourself. It is important that you speak the truth at all times—in big things and in small. God is pleased when you remain faithful and truthful.

Putting away falsehood, let all of us speak the truth to
our neighbors, for we are members of one another.

Ephesians 4:25, NRSV

The truth is incontrovertible. Panic may resent it; ignorance
may deride it; malice may distort it, but there it is.

SIR WINSTON CHURCHILL

TODAY
is the DAY...

To Resist Temptation

No temptation has overtaken you except such as is common to man; but God is faithful, who will not allow you to be tempted beyond what you are able, but with the temptation will also make the way of escape, that you may be able to bear it.

1 Corinthians 10:13, NKJV

A moment on the lips, forever on the hips. When you are tempted to take that luscious dessert, think about what happens after that moment of instant gratification. It is the same with any temptation, whether you are tempted to make a cutting remark or to cut corners. Ask God to help you make a better choice. Think of all the benefits that will come from resisting that temptation, from a trim figure to a heart at peace. Just say a simple "no thank you" to temptation's siren song.

Let your eyes look straight ahead. Keep looking right in front of you. Make level paths for your feet to walk on. Only go on ways that are firm. Don't turn to the right or left. Keep your feet from the path of evil.

Proverbs 4:25–27, NIrV

> *What is the use of running when we are not on the right road?*
> GERMAN PROVERB

TODAY
is the DAY...

To Ask for Divine Peace

A heart at peace gives life to the body.
Proverbs 14:30, NIV

*D*ivine peace in your heart and mind is not subject to the whims of circumstance and fortune. It is a true and lasting peace that grows as you learn to trust God. If your life is filled with turmoil, ask God to fill you with divine peace. Start with choosing thoughts of faith instead of fear. Look forward to your future with peace of mind. Whether your immediate circumstances change or stay the same, you can find an inner confidence and know that God will be there to see you through whatever life has in store. Know that God is by your side.

[Jesus said,] "I have come that they may have life,
and that they may have it more abundantly."

John 10:10, NKJV

We are not a postwar generation, but a
pre-peace generation. Jesus is coming.
CORRIE TEN BOOM

TODAY
is the DAY...

To Experience True Happiness

May the God of hope fill you with all joy and peace
in believing, that you may abound in hope by
the power of the Holy Spirit.

Romans 15:13, NKJV

*M*any people confuse happiness and joy. Happiness is a
temporary feeling of pleasure or contentment that fluctu-
ates according to your outward circumstances. Buying a
new car, for example, may make you happy, but when it
breaks down, you are not so happy anymore. The Bible
speaks of a lasting feeling of contentment that comes from
within and is based on your relationship with God. The
Bible refers to this as joy. It is never-changing because God
is never-changing. It is one of the evidences of His presence in your life.

I have told you this so that my joy may
be in you and that your joy may be complete.

John 15:11, NIV

Joy is the serious business of heaven.
C. S. LEWIS

TODAY
is the **DAY...**

To Receive the Gift of Mercy

He who conceals his sins does not prosper,
but whoever confesses and renounces them finds mercy.

Proverbs 28:13, NIV

*M*ercy is a gift. It is about receiving something you do not deserve and about not receiving what you do deserve. Mercy moves beyond judgment and forgives any trespasses or debts. But in God's mercy, you have an even greater gift. It is as if all your sins and failures and shortcomings have been dropped in the deep sea, and God put up a No Fishing sign. If you have been kicking yourself for what you have done—or what you have left undone—accept God's mercy, forgiveness, and love today. Give thanks for a fresh start.

Blessed are the merciful,
for they will receive mercy.

Matthew 5:7, NRSV

Jesus weeps and loves me still.
CHARLES WESLEY

TODAY
is the DAY...

To Pursue Your Dreams

The desire of the righteous will be granted.
Proverbs 10:24, NRSV

*G*od wants to help you identify those ambitions that are in accordance with His will and purpose for your life, because they will bring you the greatest degree of joy and personal fulfillment. Ask Him to firmly establish those dreams that He has placed in your heart. Your dreams will mature along with your faith. As you nurture your unique gifts and talents, and pursue that which brings you joy, you will discover that each dream is a seed that can mature into God's fruitful plan for your life.

The path of the righteous is like the light of dawn,
which shines brighter and brighter until full day.
Proverbs 4:18, NRSV

The future is as bright as the promises of God.
ADONIRAM JUDSON

TODAY
is the DAY...

TO

Take a Joy Break

·

Study the Bible

·

Pray for Understanding

·

Perform Spiritual Maintenance

·

Ask for Divine Peace

·

Pursue Your Dreams

·

Focus on Your Blessings

·

Rely on What You Know

·

Give Graciously

Inside the will of God there is no failure.
Outside the will of God there is no success.

BERNARD EDINGER

All our steps are ordered by the LORD.

Proverbs 20:24, NRSV

TODAY *is the* DAY...

To Handle Money Well

Don't spend time thinking about what you will eat or drink. Don't worry. . . . Your Father knows that you need them. But put God's kingdom first. Then those other things will also be given to you.

Luke 12:29–31, NIrV

*M*oney is neither good nor bad in and of itself. It is what you believe about money and what you do with money that count. You do not have to idolize—or demonize—it. Handle what money you do have as a trust from God, and use it well. Do not worry about how little or how much money you have. Focus on God's promise to provide what you need. Your financial status may change a number of times in your life, but God's steady hand on your life is constant.

"Bring the whole tithe into the storehouse, that there may be food in my house. Test me in this," says the LORD Almighty, "and see if I will not throw open the floodgates of heaven and pour out so much blessing that you will not have room enough for it."

Malachi 3:10, NIV

When wealth is lost, nothing is lost; when health is lost, something is lost; when character is lost, all is lost.

BILLY GRAHAM

TODAY
is the DAY...

To Focus on Your Blessings

The blessing of the LORD makes rich,
and he adds no sorrow with it.

Proverbs 10:22, NRSV

*D*id a friend give you a compliment today that made you feel good about yourself? Did a new opportunity for personal growth cross your path? Did something else happen that made your day a bit brighter? Little blessings happen every day, and they are reminders of the great blessings of God's love and tender care. Count your blessings. Take the time to focus on God's blessings both great and small, and give Him thanks and praise for all the blessings He places in your life.

Blessed be the God and Father of our Lord Jesus Christ,
who has blessed us with every spiritual blessing
in the heavenly places in Christ.

Ephesians 1:3, NAS

Myself in constant good health, and in a most handsome
and thriving condition, blessed be Almighty God for it.

SAMUEL PEPYS

TODAY
is the DAY...
To Create a Legacy

A good man leaves an inheritance to his children's children.
Proverbs 13:22, NAS

*E*veryone will leave a legacy, because you will be remembered for how you lived. You may not feel that you have accomplished anything particularly outstanding in your life, but your legacy is the sum total of who you are, the values you stand for, and the accomplishments you have managed. Create a legacy of good deeds, kindly actions, and living in integrity. You can also create a legacy by contributing to a cause that will outlive you. Ask God how you can begin creating a legacy for tomorrow in today's choices.

A righteous man who walks in his integrity—
how blessed are his sons after him.

Proverbs 20:7, NAS

Think of what impressed you about your parents. Think of the impression you are making upon your own children. That is legacy.

AUTHOR UNKNOWN

TODAY
is the **DAY...**

To Rely on What You Know

Those who work for good will find happiness.
Proverbs 12:20, GNT

*T*here is no guarantee that storm clouds will rain on everyone but you. When you are getting soaked like everyone
else, peace comes from knowing that you need not rely on
what you feel but on what you know. You know that God
is there with you through it all and that His love is sure
and certain. You know the truth that looks beyond appearances to see God's hand at work in all situations. Turn
your thoughts toward your loving Creator, and let Him
renew your reservoir of peace.

To set the mind on the Spirit is life and peace.
Romans 8:6, NRSV

---

*Peace that Jesus gives is not the absence of trouble, but is
rather the confidence that He is there with you always.*

AUTHOR UNKNOWN

TODAY
is the DAY...
To Give Graciously

One who is gracious to a poor man lends to the LORD.
Proverbs 19:17, NAS

*G*iving graciously means giving without strings attached or judging the person you are giving to. Giving graciously means that you give because you want to give, not because you expect something in return. Giving anonymously is a wonderful way to learn to give with grace. Look for a person or a cause that could benefit by your giving. Ask God to show you not only whom to give to, but how to get the gift to him or her so the person does not know who gave it. Find satisfaction in the giving itself.

[A good person] gives generously to the needy, and his kindness never fails; he will be powerful and respected.

Psalm 112:9, GNT

> *A man there was, and they called him mad;*
> *the more he gave, the more he had.*
> JOHN BUNYAN

TODAY *is the* DAY...

To Keep Building the Dream

"I know the plans I have for you," declares the LORD,
"plans to prosper you and not to harm you,
plans to give you hope and a future."

Jeremiah 29:11, NIV

*T*his is the only life you have. So dare to pursue your
dreams. Do not give up. God planted a dream in your
heart, and He will see you through as you build it.
Sometimes there are obstacles and disappointments. But
you must not allow them to stop you. Keep working on
your dreams, one step at a time. Do your best and trust
God with the rest. It may take a long time for a dream to
come to fruition, especially if it is a big dream. Trust God,
and keep dreaming.

Those who wait for the LORD will gain new strength.

Isaiah 40:31, NAS

Dreams grow holy put in action.
ADELAIDE PROCTOR

Readers who enjoyed this
book will also enjoy

NOW
is the TIME

...insights for living an
abundant life